Cultural Genocide in Tibet

A Report

The Tibet Policy Institute
The Department of Information and International Relations
Central Tibetan Administration

Published by the Tibet Policy Institute
Printed by Mahayana Press, New Delhi #+919873388032

Drafting Committee: Thubten Samphel, Bhuchung D. Sonam,
Dr. Rinzin Dorjee and Dr. Tenzin Desal

Contents

Abbreviation

TIBET   Tibet in this report refers to the entire Tibetan Plateau comprising of the three traditional Tibetan provinces of Central Tibet, Kham and Amdo. Major parts of Kham and Amdo are incorporated into various Chinese provinces such as Sichuan, Yunnan and Gansu by Beijing since its occupation of Tibet. Since then Amdo has been made into a separate province and renamed as Qinghai.

CCP   Chinese Communist Party

DMC   Democratic Management Committee

ICJ   International Commission of Jurists

ICT   International Campaign for Tibet

NATO   North Atlantic Treaty Organization

PAP   People's Armed Police

PLA   People's Liberation Army

PRC   People's Republic of China

PSB   Public Security Bureau

TAR   Tibet Autonomous Region

TCHRD   Tibetan Centre for Human and Democracy

TIN   Tibet Information Network

WRD   Western Region Development

Foreword

This report on the cultural genocide in Tibet is based on the testimonies of individual Tibetans, the writings of Tibetan, Chinese and foreign scholars, reports of the International Commission of Jurists, the resolutions of the General Assembly of UN, and the attitude of successive Chinese Communist leaders on Tibetan culture that shaped China's Tibet policy, which in turn contributed to the systematic physical and institutional destruction of the foundations of Tibetan culture.

We do not use the term cultural genocide lightly. Raphael Lemkin, who first coined the term, genocide, in 1944 in his book, *Axis Rule in Occupied Europe*, says, "By 'genocide' we mean the destruction of an ethnic group ... Generally speaking, genocide does not necessarily mean the immediate destruction of a nation, except when accomplished by mass killings of all members of a nation. It is intended rather to signify a coordinated plan of different actions aiming at the destruction of essential foundations of the life of national groups, with the aim of annihilating the groups themselves. The objectives of such a plan would be disintegration of the political and social institutions, of culture, language, national feelings, religion, and the economic existence of national groups, and the destruction of the personal security, liberty, health, dignity, and even the lives of the individuals belonging to such groups..."

Furthermore, in the initial draft of the UN Convention on Genocide prepared by the Secretary General of the UN and *ad hoc* Committee on genocide stated that "In this Convention genocide also means any deliberate act committed with the intent to destroy the language, religion or culture of a national or racial or religious group on grounds of national or racial origin or religious belief of its members." All these apply to the case of Tibet under China.

In this report we have examined four vital areas where acts of genocide have been and are still being committed. They are religion, language, the forceful removal of Tibetan nomads and China's

i

continuing population transfer onto the Tibetan Plateau. Policies relentlessly carried out in these four areas have robbed the Tibetans of their culture and language and have damaged their traditional way of life. The influx of Chinese migrant workers, facilitated by the new railway line and an administration in favour of the migrants, are reducing the Tibetans to an increasingly disenfranchised minority in their own land. We have also examined the Chinese authorities' active interference in the *tulku* system — the system of reincarnating lamas who sustain the spiritual lineage — and the authorities' disruption of the Tibetan monastic education system that have enabled the Tibetans to transmit the teachings of the Buddha to successive new generation of students. All these factors have made it beyond the ability of Tibetans in Tibet today to renew and refresh their culture.

This destruction in Tibet is borne out by prominent Tibetans, like the late Panchen Lama who in his daring and historic 70,000 character petition to the Chinese Premier Zhou Enlai in 1962 moaned the fact "religion in Tibet today has no future." There are many more distressed Tibetan voices, whose eyewitness testimonies are confirmed by Chinese scholars and independent organizations in China, who have no reason to support the Tibetans except to affirm a gross injustice. The best example of Chinese solidarity with the Tibetan people is Gongmeng, the Open Constitution Initiative, an NGO based in Beijing. In 2009, Gongmeng issued a report on the causes of the 2008 Tibet-wide peaceful protests. The report said that the protests that spread throughout Tibet that year were triggered by Beijing's hardline policies. In its recommendations to the Chinese government the report suggested that in future Beijing must base its Tibet policies on the aspirations of the people of Tibet.

China's genocidal policies in Tibet are tragically illustrated by the ongoing fiery protests that engulf Tibet today. Since 2009, 149 Tibetans have set themselves on fire. All of them have called for the return of His Holiness the Dalai Lama to Tibet and for freedom for their homeland. Till now no attempt has been made by Beijing to address the genuine grievances of the Tibetan people. Instead, China has increased repressive measures that have turned Tibet into a police state. The 2017 Freedom House report says that Tibet is one of the least free countries in the world. Beijing's oppression of the Tibetan people is whitewashed by white papers. The latest white paper on Tibet was issued by the State Council, the cabinet of the Chinese government, on 22 October 2013. Called Development and Progress of Tibet, the white paper says, "The Tibetan people have gained freedom, equality and dignity, and are enjoying the fruits of modern civilization."

If this is true, how does Beijing explain the 149 self-immolations that say there is no freedom in Tibet or why Tibet today is burning?

We are bringing out this report before the international community because the cultural genocide that is going on is the collective experience of the Tibetan people. It is also because those of us living in free societies have the moral responsibility to speak up for the Tibetans in Tibet whose collective voice has been effectively silenced.

We hope that this report will be a part of a larger effort by the international community to convince the Chinese government of the immense advantages of restoring the fundamental rights of the Tibetan people in a manner that will meet the aspirations of the Tibetan people. This also conforms to President Xi Jinping's determination to realise the China Dream.

Dr. Lobsang Sangay
Sikyong
Kashag,
Central Tibetan Administration
Dharamsala
October 2017

Executive Summary

This is a comprehensive report on the Chinese Communist Party's systematic destruction of Tibetan culture, traditional way of life and Tibetan religion since its occupation of Tibet in 1949-50, which according to Raphael Lemkin's definition is a form of cultural genocide, both in intent and purpose. The report is based on the firsthand testimonials by survivors of Chinese gulags and those who are still languishing in jails, numerous books on Tibet and its people by foreign and Chinese scholars as well as Tibetans living in and outside Tibet, research papers, leaked official documents from the People's Republic of China and reports by Human Rights Watch, International Commission of Jurists, Tibet Information Network, International Campaign for Tibet, Tibetan Centre for Human Rights & Democracy and the UN resolutions on Tibet.

This report is in two parts.

Part one defines Tibetan culture. It reveals:

— the development of Tibetan civilization with its own architecture, medical system, astrology, methods of agriculture, animal-herding, arts and language with a monumental body of literature and rich spiritual traditions

— the introduction of Buddhism from India in the seventh century and how its universal values of compassion and non-violence broadened Tibetan civilization, and the development of the monastic education system which enabled continued renewal and transmission of Buddhist teachings till 1959

Part two records the destruction of Tibetan culture as documented by scholars, jurists and the UN, and details Beijing's systematic annihilation of traditional Tibetan culture, language and religious traditions by pointing out:

— the intolerant views shown by the Chinese communist leaders towards Tibetan culture and religion based on a perceived threat to their authority and legitimacy in Tibet

— the complete destruction of Tibetan Buddhism and religious traditions leading to increased social breakdowns, lawlessness, communal disharmony, uncontrolled greed and a high growth in sex trade and alcoholism; and the collapse of the monastic education system resulting in illiteracy and a total breakdown in the transmission of Buddhist teachings from one generation to another

— the education system that is shaped by ideological viewpoint to stifle any Tibetan character, identity and content leaving little room for Tibetans growing up in Tibet to learn their language and find their cultural roots, and the increased crackdown on Tibetan intellectuals and writers because of their creative expressions

— the forceful removal of Tibetan nomads from their land and coercing them into government-built housing colonies and fencing off of pastures that has rendered their knowledge about Tibet's fragile ecosystem useless and the devastation of their lives, how the large-scale mining and other infrastructural constructions have taken over the land, tipping the ecological balance off to a point where the impact will be catastrophic

— the massive exodus of Chinese population into Tibet since the *xiafang* (downward transfer to the countryside) campaign and how Western China 'Development' Programme expedited the population transfer, the impact of this huge Chinese migrants have on the Tibetan traditional values and how it undermines Tibetan culture and marginalise the Tibetans.

Introduction

China committing cultural genocide in Tibet is an accusation easy to make and difficult to explain. The difficulty in explaining cultural genocide in Tibet stems not from the lack of evidence. In fact, there is a growing body of cultural genocide literature coming out of Tibet. The difficulty arises from the way China portrays itself to the world and how it behaves at home. China describes itself as a multi-national state but behaves as an empire, especially to the minorities. China scholars have commented on China as an empire pretending to be a nation state. The contradiction between its self-portrayal and its real imperial impulses is at the heart of China's destruction of Tibet's Buddhist civilization.

No one can fault China on the rights granted to its national minorities on paper. Article 2 of the constitution of the People's Republic of China declares, "All power in the People's Republic of China belongs to the people."

On regional autonomy, article 4 says, "Regional autonomy is practiced in areas where people of minority nationalities live in compact communities; in these areas organs of self-government are established for the exercise of the right of autonomy."

Article 119 has this to say, "The organs of self-government of the national autonomous areas independently administer educational, scientific, cultural, public health and physical culture affairs in their respective areas, sort out and protect the cultural legacy of the nationalities and work for the development and prosperity of their cultures."

On the right to use one's language, spoken and written, article 121 says, "In performing their functions, the organs of self-government of the national autonomous areas, in accordance with the autonomy regulations of the respective areas, employ the spoken and written language or languages in common use in the locality."

All these rights granted to the minorities on paper will do any liberal democracy proud. The Tibetans have no quarrel with the constitution of the People's Republic of China. The Tibetan argument is that what is enshrined in the constitution should be fully implemented on the ground.

The bigger Tibetan argument is based on the Tibetan perception of the Chinese Communist Party's visceral attitude to Tibetan culture. The party leaders' gut feeling towards Tibetan culture is expressed in close-door meetings. The overall attitude of the party leaders to Tibet's distinct culture and identity is that the very existence of Tibetan culture is a basis for Tibet spinning out of control. At close-door meetings, some Tibet party secretaries are known to have expressed the opinion that the autonomous region should be incorporated into Chinese provinces like Sichuan and the very name of Tibet should be wiped off the face of the earth. Zhang Qingli, the Tibet party secretary from 2006 to 2011 said, "The Communist Party is like parents to the Tibetan people and are always considerate about what the children need. The Party is the real Buddha for the Tibetans." In 2011, Zhang Qingli described the Dalai Lama as "a wolf in monk's robes, a devil with a human face and but the heart of a beast."

Such virulent depiction of the Tibetan leader shapes the Party's overall attitude to Tibet's Buddhist culture and this innate hostility is demonstrated in the ongoing bout of destruction at Larung Gar, a sprawling centre of learning in eastern Tibet. Thousands of monks and nuns have been expelled from the academy and their homes destroyed. Such assault on the physical manifestation of their faith is viewed by the Tibetan people as an assault on the core values of their spiritual heritage. The Party's true intentions in Tibet are also revealed in the forced re-location of millions of nomads, in the rapid urbanisation in Tibet, the transformation of many Tibetan towns into so many Chinatowns and the encouragement of mass tourism from the mainland in the hope that many of these Chinese tourists will settle in Tibet.

Scholarly Debate on Ethnic Policies

China's policy to its minorities came under scholarly discussion in the wake of the peaceful protests that erupted throughout Tibet in 2008 and the violence that broke out in Urumqi in Xinjiang in 2009. In the aftermath of these events, an increasing number of Chinese academics consider China's current minority policy too lenient and forms the basis for the dismemberment of the country along ethnic lines like the former Soviet Union and Yugoslavia. Academics like Ma Rong of Peking University and Hu Angang of Tsinghua University recommended a "second generation" of ethnic policies that would encourage China's minorities to integrate more fully with the Han Chinese majority through inter-marriage, social interaction and the use of the Chinese language. These scholars called for the removal of ethnic identity for each of the minorities and their fusion with the majority Han Chinese population.

Some scholars have argued that "the policy of regional ethnic autonomy is a disguised form of ethnic segregation." Li Datong, a liberal Chinese intellectual, said "the root cause of all ethnic problems today is the way we emphasize and strengthen ethnic differences."

In 2012, Zhu Weiqun, then the executive director of the United Front Work Department, joined the call for the "second generation" ethnic policies and recommended the removal of ethnic status from identification cards, a freeze on any new ethnic autonomous units, ethnically mixed schooling and strengthening of Chinese language education.

Some ultra-nationalist Chinese have recommended that the Tibet Autonomous Region is too large and should be broken into smaller autonomous units. Some of these smaller units should be merged into neighbouring provinces.

This open, public debate on China's ethnic policies is unprecedented. In all previous years since the founding of the People's Republic of China discussion on ethnic policies is the preserve of the party-state. Allowing this explosion of debate on China's ethnic policies on online platforms was perhaps to gauge public opinion on this burning issue.

The party-state's response to the debate for the moment is that the eruption of protests and violence in China's ethnic regions is not a sign of the failure of ethnic policies but interference from outside. At least publicly the party-state insists that its ethnic policies are working and are successful.

China's Real Plans for Tibet

Urbanization

However, behind the scenes, one suspects that the party-state has big plans for Tibet. One plan is the urbanization of Tibet. According to Tibetan researchers in exile, China has so far managed to urbanize 13 Tibetan regions. They are Lhasa, Shigatse, Nyingtri, Lhoka and Tsethang in central Tibet. In Kham, the urbanized regions are Chamdo, Yushu, Dartsedo and Dechen. In Amdo the urbanized regions are Xining, Tsoshar, Gormo, Terlenkha and Tso. According to Tenzin Dheten, formerly of the Tibet Policy Institute and now head of the China Desk of the Department of Information and International Relations of the Central Tibetan Administration, China has three main objectives for the urbanization of Tibet. They are "to encourage mass population transfer of Han Chinese into these regions, to assimilate Tibetans and to extract rich natural resources in these regions of Tibet."

In this way, China is planning in Tibet what it has done so successfully in Manchuria, Inner Mongolia and what it is currently doing in Xinjiang - flooding these regions with Han Chinese settlers and making them the dominant ethnic population. One report says, "China is systematically underreporting the number of ethnic Chinese migrant workers arriving in Lhasa every year who could be outnumbering and overwhelming the number of Tibetans living in the capital. The expanding railway line in Tibet, the network of all-weather highways and improved and expanding air traffic is making this possible. The overall objective of this strategy is to bind Tibet more closely to the Chinese mainland.

Mass Domestic Tourism in Tibet

To complement this strategy, China is encouraging mass tourism in Tibet. Chinese government says this year alone 23 million Chinese tourists will visit Tibet. This means 63,000 Chinese tourists arrive in the Tibet Autonomous Region every day. Chinese authorities say the numbers will rise to 35 million visitors by 2020.

Tourism is considered a pillar industry of Tibet. Tourism makes up one-fifth of the total economy of the Tibet Autonomous Region. So far, it has created 320,000 jobs.

Some reports dispute the figure of 23 million Chinese tourists visiting Tibet this year alone. They estimate that there are not enough trains, planes, buses to transport 23 million Chinese visitors to Tibet every year. These reports say that there are also not enough hotels and beds to accommodate and host 23 million visitors.

Whatever the truth, the number of Chinese tourists visiting Tibet is massive. Media reports say that at the Lhasa train station six trains from China arrive every day. In the peak season each train transports 800 to 1,000 passengers. In the low season one train carries 300 to 500 passengers. Likewise, there are between 53 to 58 passenger flights arriving in Lhasa from China every day.

Tibetans in Tibet say that China's massive and growing domestic tourism in Tibet is helping Beijing bind Tibet more closely to China, trivializing Tibetan culture, marginalizing the Tibetan people and polluting Tibet's pristine environment. China's active encouragement of domestic tourism in Tibet is in part sparked by the hope that many Chinese tourists will settle in Tibet, far from the urban congestion and pollution of the mainland.

China's Plan to Appoint the Next Dalai Lama

However, China's biggest plan for Tibet is one of wait and see. China is waiting for the passing away of His Holiness the Dalai Lama and to appoint the next Dalai Lama. It is confident that time is on its side and it has the resources to impose the next Dalai Lama on the Tibetan people and the world.

In thinking this China is making its biggest mistake. Already more than 149 Tibetans have set themselves on fire because of China's refusal to allow His Holiness the Dalai Lama to visit Tibet. Till now the Tibetan people kept their struggle non-violent in deference to the wishes of His Holiness the Dalai Lama. In brushing aside the present Dalai Lama and preparing to appoint the next one all in the hope that Beijing can handle the Tibetan people, the Chinese authorities are travelling on the road to the destabilization of Tibet.

Amidst all this doom and gloom, there is some hope that President Xi Jinping might have one or two surprises up his sleeve.

More than the Party's assault on monasteries and dwelling places of monks and nuns, what is hurting and humiliating the Tibetan people the most is the Party assault on Tibet's spiritual space and its attempt to dominate the Buddhist lineage tree. Like manufacturing facts on the ground in the South China Sea, the Party is manufacturing facts in Tibet's spiritual space. The Party is arrogating to itself the right to recognise and appoint Tibet's spiritual masters.

The Party's assault on Tibetan Buddhism is on two fronts. One assault is on Tibetan Buddhism's lineage tree. The unbroken lineage tree of the four schools of Tibetan Buddhism traces its sanctity to the Buddha himself and down the centuries from masters to students to the present Tibetan Buddhist lamas. In this process, successive masters not only guide his students in their spiritual development by explaining the teachings of the Buddha and the commentaries made on these teachings by later masters but also empower their students to pass on these teachings to others. The students' ability to trace what they learn right to the top of the lineage tree, the Buddha himself, gives what they learn sanctity and spiritual potency.

By maintaining a data base of Party-approved Tibetan reincarnating lamas and arrogating to itself the right to appoint Buddhist masters, the Party is uprooting the Buddhist lineage tree.

The Party's second assault is on the concept of reincarnation. The Buddhist concept of reincarnation started in India. But out of all the countries to which Buddhism spread, Tibet was the only country which carried out the concept of reincarnating lamas. And Tibetan Buddhists believe enlightened beings can choose the place and time of his or her rebirth through their own individual spiritual efforts through many lifetimes. The ability to reincarnate and where and when is an individual's private choice, beyond the decision of the Party.

At the top of the Tibetan pantheon of enlightened beings sits Avalokiteshevara, the Bodhisattva of Compassion who Tibetans believe is the protector of Tibet and in his human form is manifested in the Dalai Lamas of Tibet. The Party's plea to the 14th Dalai Lama, couched in the language of a stern order, to reincarnate may mean the Chinese Communist Party believes in the concept of reincarnation which violates Party ideology. Or this blatant grab at Tibet's spiritual space is an implicit admission by the Party that it cannot rule Tibet without the Dalai Lamas. The only way forward is for the Party to take the hand extended by the Dalai Lama and resolve not only the issue of Tibet but all the contradictions the Party has wrapped itself in.

PART ONE

A CULTURE OF COMPASSION

The Tibetans developed a unique civilization with its own architecture and bridge-building, astrology and calendar, medical system, methods of agriculture and animal-herding, sciences and arts, a monumental body of literature, both oral and written, and rich spiritual traditions. This civilization was immensely enriched when Tibetans from the 7th to the 12th century consciously and comprehensively transmitted the whole body of the wisdom of ancient India to Tibet. The incorporation of Buddhism with its universal values of compassion and non-violence into Tibetan culture broadened the appeal of Tibetan civilization, bringing into its orbit non-Tibetans scattered across vast distances. This event transformed how Tibet's social order was organized, the nature of its state power and how the country conducted its diplomacy.

A civilization is invariably a product of conquest of others. On the other hand, Tibetan civilization that came into being, especially after the Tibetan people's embrace of Buddhism, is one based on the conquest of the self. On this point, no other people have pursued the idea of inner conquest and transformation with the same intensity as the Tibetans did. It can be arguably stated that Tibet was one of the few civilizations that put the resources of the state in the service of the clergy to pursue and practice the idea of inner transformation. After having taken this idea of self-conquest from India, the Tibetans undertook a stupendous translation effort and instituted monasteries all over Tibet devoted to the study and practice of inner transformation.

The enduring contribution of this civilization to humanity is its creation of the institutions needed to study, understand and use the tools of inner or spiritual technology developed by the Buddha to overcome human suffering and its ability to make available the material means and establish the spiritual environment to transform individuals into happier and more productive human beings. These

1

institutions were established so that every single practitioner had all the resources available that were essential to develop and expand compassion for the benefit of all sentient beings. These institutions helped the practitioners to come to a better understanding of the nature of impermanence, life and death.

The spiritual techniques taught in the monasteries and the Tibetans' absolute devotion to the cultivation and practice of compassion became central to their culture and shaped their subsequent historical development. This culture of compassion has been helped in its development by the Tibetans' innate sense of the spiritual sanctity of their land and their reverence for the natural environment. This has contributed to making Tibetan civilization environmentally friendly and economically sustainable on the world's highest and largest and yet ecologically fragile plateau.

It took the Tibetans about five centuries to translate, study and disseminate the teachings of the Buddha within Tibet. In their book, *A Cultural History of Tibet*, David Snellgrove and Hugh Richardson consider this transmission "one of the greatest deliberate importations of a foreign culture in which any country has ever engaged." This mighty enterprise, stretching from the 7th to 12th century, was undertaken by countless Tibetan scholars, equipped with unbelievable commitment and super-human energy, under the guidance and scholarly supervision of some of the greatest Indian masters of the day.

After having taken firm roots in Tibet, this culture of compassion, with its exuberant and liberating message that every human being is a potential Buddha, spread to all directions in and outside Tibet. Scholars and students, risking life and limb, traversed enormous distances to study Buddhism in the monasteries of Tibet. They came from regions that today comprise of Mongolia, Buryatia and Tuva, Kalmykia stretched along the Caspian Sea in Russia, the Buddhist Himalayas, like Ladakh, Lahaul and Spiti, Sikkim and Arunachal Pradesh in India, Mustang, Dolpo and Solo Kumbu in Nepal, and Bhutan. Though the spatial spread of Tibetan civilization in itself is amazing, what is more remarkable is the devotion of non-Tibetans to the font of their cultural wellspring in Tibet. In this way, Tibet became the centre of learning for the countries and regions in which Tibetan Buddhist civilization took root and blossomed.

In her book, So *Close to Heaven: The Vanishing Buddhist Kingdoms of the Himalayas*, Barbara Crossette, a veteran reporter of the *New York Times*, describes ancient Tibet in these words.

"For a few hundred years, in the seventh and eight centuries, a Tibetan empire strong enough to box in the Tang dynasty of China on the western flank flourished in the landlocked heart of Asia. Tibetan armies advanced and retreated from bases on the Tibetan plateau; Himalayan monks and soldiers traded influences with Buddhists of other schools, reinforcing a cosmopolitan culture...From the vantage point of our era, Tibet may appear to be a sad civilization long stripped of the glories it enjoyed and the power it wielded more than a thousand years ago...We who encounter Tibet at the end of the twentieth century thus marvel at even what little we can discover of its glorious medieval history."

The development of Tibetan culture was a long-drawn process. The Western stereotype of Tibet as being "forbidden," "isolated" and a Shangri-la, with its implication of being remote and quite out of this world, is false. Tibet in the past was an active, sometimes a dominant, player in the cross-cultural pollination of Asia. Ancient Tibet energetically drew rich and diverse cultural influences as far afield as Iran, possibly Greece and Rome, Central Asia, India, China and Burma through present-day Yunnan province. Because of the open-minded outlook of the ancient Tibetans, Tibet became a culture with the ability to continually refresh and make itself relevant to any given period and condition in its long history.

In this brief introduction, it is not possible to identify all the elements that make the edifice called Tibetan civilization. However, the following are some of the main building-blocks that constitute the architecture of Tibet's civilization and culture.

3

The Land

Tibet is the heart of Asia. Like the human heart, it is surrounded by ribs, the mountains. Like the human heart it pumps blood, the major river systems that sustain life in Asia. Tibet is the highest plateau in the world. Because of its scarce and rarefied air, Tibet sucks in air from the surrounding regions, thus in effect becoming the primary cause for the monsoon of South Asia. Tibet is also the world's largest and highest plateau.

Today Chinese scientists call Tibet the 'Water Tower of Asia" because six of Asia's major river systems have their source in the Tibetan highlands to bring life-giving water to the whole of South Asia, China and a large part of South-east Asia. The rivers from Tibet flow through diverse countries such as Pakistan, India, Nepal, Bhutan, Bangladesh, China, Burma, Thailand, Vietnam, Laos, and Cambodia and contribute to the livelihood of millions of people in Asia.

Even more recently Chinese scientists refer to Tibet as the "Third Pole", since Tibet has the largest concentration of glaciers, outside the two Poles, which feed these rivers.

Language and Literature

Linguists assign the Tibetan language to the Tibeto-Burman group of languages and further trace its origins to the Sino-Tibetan language group, which is recognized as an important language group of the world. Whatever the case, variations of the Tibetan language are spoken in many pockets of the Himalayan region from Ladakh in the west, Arunachal Pradesh in the east and along the Sino-Tibetan borderlands inhabited previously by Ch'iang, Moso or Naxi and the ancient Tanguts or the Xi Xia people.

Tibetan language as a tool of communication over this huge landmass was strengthened when in the 7th century Thomi Sambhota invented the written script based on the Indian Gupta and Brahmi alphabets. According to *A History of Traditional Fields of Learning: A Concise*

4

History of Dissemination of Traditional Fields of Learning written by the late Tibetan scholar Muge Samten and translated into English by Sangye Tendar Naga, King Songtsen Gampo "sent sixteen people, including Thonmi Sambhota and Taglo Dhetrong, to India to study various religions, languages and literature... When he returned to Tibet ... he devised the first Tibetan script and established the tradition of written Tibetan...it became the root of all knowledge."

The common written script of the Tibetan language enabled the Tibetan people to store the whole body of the wisdom of Buddhist India. The script also enabled the Tibetans to store and leave for posterity non-Buddhist knowledge and sciences emanating from other cultural realms. Above all, the script reinforced the basic cultural unity of the Tibetan people and cemented the common identity of the inhabitants of the Land of Snow.

R.A. Stein, the author of *Tibetan Civilization,* describes the efforts made by the Tibetan people to put the script into use as "prodigious". He says, "Tibetan literature is absolutely vast, and we are far from having a complete inventory of it." He divides Tibetan literature into written and oral, indigenous and non-indigenous. By "non-indigenous" Stein is obviously referring to the body of work translated into Tibetan from the Buddhist canons of India. Stein adds that subjects dealt in the body of work of Tibetan literature are nearly all religious and philosophical, except for a few treatises on the traditional sciences, grammar, astrology and medicine.

Stein says that Tibet's prolific scholars "very soon produced a large number of original treatises on philosophy...historical works, textbooks of grammar and prosody, dictionaries-Sanskrit-Tibetan, or vocabularies of technical terms and old words-treatises on chronological computation, astrology, divination and medicine, bibliographies, geographical descriptions and pilgrims' guides, accounts of travel—real or mystical—treatises on the art of government and on various techniques (agriculture, making of statues, china, tea, etc.)

Then there is the literature produced within the Bonpo tradition, not forgetting the oral literary tradition of folk stories like the epic of the Gesar of Ling, reportedly the longest epic in the world, comparable in its influence to the Iliad of Greece and the Mahabharata and Ramayana of India, and the literary contributions of the Tibetan Muslims, especially that of Kache Phalu.

Bonism

The two religions that had a profound influence on the Tibetan people are Bonism and Buddhism. Some scholars say Bon was homegrown in Tibet in Zhang Zhung in the neighbourhood of Mount Kailash. Others say it came from farther afield, from Tazig, sometimes identified as Persia, or which may be present Tajikistan. Whatever the case, Bon was the dominant spiritual and cultural force among Tibetans before the advent of Buddhism in Tibet.

According to Bon scholars, Bon originated in the land of Olmo Lungring, a part of a larger country called Tazig. The founder of the Bon tradition was Shenrab Miwo. The first Bon sacred texts were brought to Zhang Zhung by the six disciples of Mucho Demdrug, the successor of Shenrab Miwo. They were first translated into Zhang Zhung language and later into Tibetan. The works included in the Bon canon were written in Tibetan but a number of them, especially the older ones, retain the titles and at times passages in Zhang Zhung language.

Buddhism

The other spiritual and cultural force that fundamentally shaped the Tibetan people was Buddhism, which was introduced to Tibet during the reign of Songtsen Gampo in the 7th century. Buddhism is credited with civilizing the "ignorant" Tibetans and tempering their warlike character with the Buddhist contemplative way of life. Buddhism was introduced to Tibet in two stages, first from the 7th to the 9th century. This period of introduction is called the early transmission of Buddhism. The later transmission took place from the 11th century with the appearance in Tibet of Atisha, and other

Buddhist masters of India.

It took successive Tibetan Buddhist scholars from the 7th to the 12th century to translate and absorb the whole body of Buddhist canon. The challenge for the new generation of scholars was what to do with this vast body of translated work. Although other scholars were involved in this Herculean task, the Tibetan primarily associated in this endeavour of cataloguing, systematizing and finally compiling the Tibetan Buddhist canon of *Kagyur* (the teachings of the Buddha) and the *Tengyur* (commentaries on the teachings) was Buton (1290-1364). Snellgrove and Richardson consider this achievement as the 'apotheosis' of Tibetan scholarship and an enduring legacy of the collective and tireless efforts of Tibetan scholars down the ages.

This absorption of Buddhism into the spiritual and cultural life of Tibet enabled the Tibetan people to consistently produce a large number of Buddhist masters and scholars whose teachings and writings have enriched Tibetan civilization. This enabled the Tibetans to establish monasteries that became centres of learning, and which dominated the spiritual and intellectual life of Tibet and beyond.

Out of the Tibetans' complete devotion to Buddhism and their single-minded pursuit of the Buddhist teachings emerged two important features that were to shape the character of Tibetan civilization. One was the emergence of the monasteries and the monastic education system. These monasteries not only dominated Tibetan intellectual and spiritual life but they were soon to become a political force to be reckoned with, either collectively or individually. The monastic system served as magnets for the best minds of Tibet, who consistently produced a vast amount of scholarly and spiritual work that built upon the Buddhist spiritual heritage.

The other was putting into practice the Buddhist concept of reincarnation, when the Karma Kagyu School started the tradition of reincarnating lamas. Soon the other schools of Tibetan Buddhism adopted this practice and reincarnated lamas proliferated in Tibet and spread beyond. This had two important effects. Installing a reincarnated lama in a monastery gave it enormous prestige, not the least being the increased flow of offerings from the devotees. The other was the practice of reincarnating lamas became a unique system of leadership training for lamas at a very young age. Under strict monastic discipline and the watchful eye of committed tutors, the young reincarnated lamas blossomed into great masters. The practice of discovering reincarnated lamas was a form of "electing" spiritual leaders with the added advantage that this practice was sanctified by the full weight of Tibetan Buddhism and its legitimising force. This system is essential for the spiritual practitioners to transmit the accumulated wisdom of the lamas to the new reincarnations who in turn would teach these to their followers.

Sciences

Buddhism's taking firm roots in Tibet contributed to the development of other aspects of Tibetan culture, particularly the sciences and arts. The Buddhist treatises on the five major and five minor sciences informed and served as an impetus for those Tibetans specializing in the fields of medicine, astrology, architecture, crafts, bridge-building, performing arts, woodblock printing and other fields of human endeavour and knowledge.

Buddhism had an important impact on the development and evolution of the Tibetan medical system. Tibetan physicians say that there was a native Tibetan medical system before the advent of Buddhism. Dr Tsering Thakchoe Drungtso says, "Bon, with its own medical tradition, was the indigenous religion of Tibet ... Master Shenrab Miwo, the founder of Bon religion ... revealed the teachings of the medical texts ... and other medical treatises to his son and eight sages on their request."

The first international conference on medicine in Tibet was held during the reign of King Trisong Detsen (730-785 AD). This was attended by physicians from India, China, Persia, Nepal and Central Asia. The Elder Yuthog Yonten Gonpo (708-833 AD) was a prominent presence at the conference. He synthesized the Tibetan,

Indian, Chinese and other medical systems and came up with a treatise called *Gyud-zhi (The Four Tantras)*, though the authorship of this treatise is disputed. Some scholars attribute the authorship of this treatise to the Buddha himself.

Dr Drungtso says that Lochen Rinchen Sangpo (958-1055 AD) translated many Indian medical texts into Tibetan. Other figures who made valuable contributions to the development of the Tibetan medical practice and system were the Great Fifth Dalai Lama, who established three medical schools in Tibet and Desi Sangye Gyatso who wrote a great deal of medical treatises that are of value because of their accuracy and depth. In short, along with their ability of keeping intact the entirety of the teachings of the Buddha, the Tibetan medical tradition is an important contribution of the Tibetan people to the well-being of humanity.

Environmental Protection

One feature of Tibetan culture is the innate respect and reverence for the natural environment that the Tibetans had been handed down from ancient times. Bon considered lakes, rivers and other sources of water and mountain passes sacred. This ancient respect for nature was reinforced when Buddhism became the main faith of the Tibetan people. Buddhism believes in the interdependence of all things.

This respect for the natural habitat and all the creatures sustained by it was reflected in Tibetan government policy. When the fifth Dalai Lama assumed political power in 1642, he issued an edict for the protection of animals and the environment. An environmental decree issued by the reigning regent Tagdra in 1940 reads: "From this Iron-Dragon year, the Tibetan government has decreed that in each and every village and town in Tibet on every 8th, 15th and 30th day of each month, the 4th day of the 6th month, the 22nd day of the 9th month and the 25th day of the 10th month, no domestic animals should be killed for the purpose of selling their meat for profit or food."

9

This shows that Tibet was one of the first countries in the world that enacted environmental protection laws.

The Origin and Evolution of Tibetan Culture

In his book, *The Necklace of gZi: A Cultural History of Tibet,* Namkai Norbu, who was a professor at the University of Naples and taught Tibetan language and cultural history, says that Tibet as an organized culture and society can be traced back to 3000 years. Other scholars say Tibet's traditional mode of farming and pastoralism is at least two thousand years old and identify the origin of the Tibetan people "among the nomadic, non-Chinese Qiang tribes, who herded sheep and cattle in eastern Central Asia up to the furthest north-west borders of China many centuries before the Christian era."

In their work, *A Cultural History of Tibet*, David Snellgrove and Hugh Richardson say, "The legacy of this origin is seen in the extensive nature of Tibetan farming with its ever-present element of animal husbandry...Tibetan-speaking peoples seem to have made their way ever further westwards across the southern part of the Tibetan uplands round about the beginning of the Christian era. This is confirmed to some extent by literary sources which enable us to trace the movement of certain important clans from north-eastern Tibet to the centre of the country. The early advance of Tibetan-speaking people westwards and southwards through the Himalayas and into what is now northern and central Nepal is also confirmed by the persistence in these areas of ancient dialects of Tibetan origin."

Tibetan tradition identifies Nyatri Tsenpo (127 BC) as Tibet's first king. Before this, as mentioned in the previous section, there existed an older tradition of Bon. Namkhai Norbu says in *Drung, Deu and Bon: Narrations, Symbolic Languages and the Bon Tradition in Ancient Tibet* that the kingdom of Zhang Zhung, which was the home of Bon, had its capital at one time in Khyunglung in the vicinity of Gangkar Tise or Mount Kailash. Namkhai Norbu writes, "The centre of the kingdom of Zhang Zhung lay in what is now the region of Guge in western Tibet but its dominion spread over practically all the territory encompassed in central and eastern Tibet." Bon's cultural ideas and beliefs shaped the mind of peoples of Sumpa, Asha, Minyak and the Yarlung valley from which emerged the kings and emperors who laid the foundation of the Tibetan empire.

The Emergence of the Yarlung Dynasty

The one event which had the greatest impact on the subsequent cultural development of Tibet was the emergence of the kings of Yarlung who over the centuries cemented the peoples of the plateau under one single central authority and overran regions beyond Tibet. The ability of the kings of Yarlung, headquartered in Tsethang, the cradle of Tibetan civilization, to bring the whole plateau under one administration provided not only the material base for Tibet's cultural development but also the governance that strengthened the cohesion of the Tibetan people.

According to Buddhist historians, on this scene, emerged Nyatri Tsenpo in around 127 BC. From this period to the 7th century AD, until the emergence of Songtsen Gampo, who consolidated the realm of his forefathers and then took Tibet on an expansionist mission, Yarlung was ruled by a succession of thirty-one kings. During the reign of these kings, Bon remained the dominant belief system, although tentative contacts with Buddhism were made, especially during the reign of Lhatho Thori Nyentsen, the 28th king, who in around 233 AD received two Buddhist sutras which, though treated with great reverence, remained a mystery because Tibetans at the time had not mastered other peoples' languages, including Sanskrit, the language in which the two sutras were presumably written. This piece of scriptural wisdom from Buddhist India remained as the *Nyenpo Sangwa*, A Fragile Secret.

Songtsen Gampo and the Unification of Tibet

One of the great figures in Tibetan history, Songtsen Gampo, was born in 617. His reign was characterized by an outburst of military adventures within and beyond Tibet. In 634, the Tibetans subdued the Tuyu-hun (Turco-Mongols) camped around Tso Nyonpo or

11

Kokonor Lake. In his study of Tibetan history, *Tibet: A Political History*, Tsepon W.D. Shakabpa writes "Meanwhile, the Tibetans had conquered parts of upper Burma and, in 640 occupied Nepal... In 643, Likme, King of Shangshung, became a vassal of the Tibetan ruler."

Commenting on Songtsen Gampo's reign, Snellgrove and Richardson write, "In a surprisingly short time, using their new subjects as allies, the Tibetans were ranging from the plains of India and the mountains of Nepal to the frontiers of China; they may even have already established contact through their new Shang-shung subject-allies with Khotan and the great international trade route that passed through it on the south side of the Takla-makan. To Tang China *Srong-brtsan-sgam-po* became a presence on their borders, to be viewed with apprehension and seriously reckoned with. His friendship was won by the grant of a Chinese princess as bride (640 AD) and his reign, which lasted till his natural death in 650 AD, was one of such exuberant military prowess and such personal prestige that it established the kingship on a firm basis and prepared it for two centuries of stable succession and almost imperial greatness."

The First Spread of Buddhism in Tibet

Songtsen Gampo's empire-building military operations indicate a desire to strengthen the cohesion of the Tibetan-speaking people and hunger for territory. These operations also indicate a far deeper hunger, hunger for new ideas. The Tibetans' contacts with different peoples and cultures whetted their appetite for new ideas and institutions that would underpin their new domain.

India welcomed the Tibetans who showed up at the feet of many Buddhist masters and extended enormous co-operation to Tibetan scholars and students in their study and mastery of the languages and wisdom held in them. After Thonmi Sambhota returned to Tibet to invent the Tibetan script, the Tibetans began the translation effort that enabled them to introduce the whole body of Buddhist wisdom to Tibet. The new script also enabled Songtsen Gampo to codify and promulgate laws. Songtsen Gampo was encouraged in his embrace of Buddhism by his Nepalese and Chinese queens, both devout Buddhists, who had each brought with them a statue of the Buddha, reportedly blessed by the Buddha himself, and constructed the temples of Jokhang and Ramoche to house these statues. Indian, Nepalese and Chinese Buddhist masters were invited to Tibet to assist in the translation effort and many Buddhist temples sprung up.

Despite some court resistance here and there in the form of individual ministers to the royal fascination with Buddhism, all the successors of Songtsen Gampo carried out his work of the study of Buddhism and translation of Buddhist texts. The next king who made contribution to the dissemination of Buddhism in Tibet was Tridey Tsugten or Mey Agzom, who reigned from 704 to 754 AD. According to Muge Samten, "During his reign, many ordained monks came from Khotan (Liyul), and many monk scholars arrived from China. They translated texts on different aspects of the dharma, healing treatises and other books...To house these texts the king constructed five temples."

The Tibetan attempt to master Buddhism was given a fresh burst of energy because after Songtsen Gampo's death, his successors wrested the oasis towns of Khotan, Kucha, Karashar and Kashgar in Turkestan from Chinese control. All these towns were centres of Buddhist learning and it was along this route that Buddhism made its way to China before it came to Tibet. Scholars and monks from these towns assisted Tibetan scholars in the study and translation of Buddhist scriptural wisdom.

Trisong Detsen, 755 to 798 AD, under the guidance of Shantarakshita, the abbot of Nalanda, and Padmasambhava, constructed the great monastic university of Samye dedicated to the study of Buddhism and training of monks. According to Shakabpa, Tibetan troops were dispatched to India to recover a relic of the Buddha from Bodh Gaya, which was installed in the monastery to sanctify it. Muge Samten says that at this monastery, "several youths studied treatises on Sanskrit grammar as well as the languages of China,

Nepal, Zahor, Kashmir and Khotan. They were also trained in many other subjects and the majority of them became great scholars. Later many of them attained the skills of translators." The monastery was divided into different departments devoted to the study of different disciplines.

Snellgrove and Richardson write, "Thanks to this new impetus, Buddhism, hitherto suspect as a dangerous foreign influence, began to become a truly Tibetan religion, and there followed a surge of activity in the translation of Indian and Chinese Buddhists texts into Tibetan."

The construction of the great monastery was followed by the holding of the great debate between Kamalashila, a student of Shantarakshita, and the Chinese Buddhist Mahayana on the correct path to attain enlightenment. Kamalashila advocated that the only way to attain Buddhahood was the gradual and long process of acquisition of knowledge and accumulation of merit. The Chinese case of instantaneous enlightenment, according to Snellgrove and Richardson, "concentrated upon the absolute nature of buddhahood, which could be realized by any practitioner who established himself in the state of complete repose. According to this, conventional morality and intellectual endeavour are irrelevant, and in some cases even directly harmful, if they obstruct the pure contemplation of the emptiness of all concepts whatsoever."

Trisong Detsen declared that Kamalashila had won the debate and decreed that the doctrine supported and articulated by the Indians must be studied and followed in Tibet. His edict declared Buddhism the state religion. Since then Tibetans followed Indian monasticism as developed and practised in Nalanda, the great Buddhist monastic university in northern India.

Tri Ralpachen, the last of the three great kings, who according to scholars, lived or ruled from 815 to 838 or from 817 to 836. He signed a peace treaty with China in 821-822. He invited many scholars from India and there was a surge of translation works. The

Indian masters and the Tibetan translators set the standard on the rules and terms in translation, which facilitated the translation effort and made the translated texts clear and comprehensible to students. A joint effort by Indian scholars and Tibetan translators produced the first Sanskrit-Tibetan dictionary.

Tri Ralpachen's devotion to Buddhism and his strong support and the favours he granted the Buddhist clergy aroused strong opposition, culminating in his assassination. His elder brother, Langdarma, took the throne. He was said to have suppressed Buddhism with an iron-fist. Buddhist masters and scholars fled east and north-east to Kham and Amdo where the teachings of the Buddha were nurtured and kept strong. Later, Langdarma fell a victim to an assassin's arrow. There followed a succession dispute between competing heirs. This internal chaos coupled with external military attacks brought the collapse of central authority and with it the end of the Tibetans' empire-building enterprise. The collapse of central authority in Tibet constituted a huge setback for the propagation of Buddhism in Tibet but this did not dampen the Tibetan people's ardour for the teachings of the Buddha. In fact, in a way, as we will see later, the collapse of central authority in Tibet inadvertently allowed the Tibetans to use the same energy and talent they displayed in creating an empire in building a civilization.

The Second Spread of Buddhism

Although Buddhism fell into dilapidation in central Tibet, it was the established religion in Kham and Amdo in the east and northeast and in western Tibet. That was the reason why, three monks, when they learned of the suppression of Buddhism in central Tibet fled to Amdo. These three monks were Tsang Rabsel, Yo Gejung and Mar Shakyamuni. The nomads of Amdo supplied them with all their needs in return for spiritual instructions. The propagation of Buddhism in eastern Tibet was also strengthened by the efforts of the Indian teacher Smriti who "initiated the translation of new sets of tantric texts," according to Snellgrove and Richardson. In this way, eastern Tibet played an important role in the renaissance of

15

Buddhism in Tibet.

Meanwhile, western Tibet was equally active in dispatching students to India to receive teachings and inviting Indian scholars to the country. The efforts made by Tibetans in eastern and western Tibet to propagate Buddhism have been described, according to Shakabpa, as "a spark rekindled in the east spread by the wind blowing from the west."

The towering figures in western Tibet's attempt to revive Buddhism were Lhalama Yeshi O and the great and prodigious translator Rinchen Sangpo (958-1055). Lhalama Yeshe O, the king of western Tibet, dispatched twenty-one students to Kashmir to learn Sanskrit and study the Buddhist doctrine. Only two survived the rigours of the journey. They were Rinchen Sangpo and Lekpe Sherab, who became great translators and on their way back to Tibet invited Indian scholars to accompany them home. Rinchen Sangpo, in particular, is credited with making three visits to India, during which he spent about 17 years, receiving teachings from various Buddhist traditions, acquiring texts and learning the methods of spiritual practice. Rinchen Sangpo organised the building of numerous monasteries and temples where students studied the various disciplines of Buddhism. Some of these monasteries, like Tabo, stand to this day.

Lhalama Yeshi O also invited Atisha, the abbot of the university of Vikramsila in north India, to Tibet to clear up the doctrinal confusion in Tibet and to further spread the teachings. Atisha refused the invitation, saying he was needed at Vikramasila by his students. Atisha, realising the huge trouble the Tibetans underwent to take him to their country, accepted the second invitation made at the behest of Jangchub O, the nephew of Lhalama Yeshi O. Atisha, with his twenty-four disciples, and his attendants, travelled to western Tibet through Nepal and visited Tholing monastery, where Rinchen Sangpo, was the abbot.

Atisha visited Samye, the monastery established during Trisong Detsen's reign. According to Shakabpa, he reportedly exclaimed

16

that he had never seen such an extensive and thorough system of translation of Buddhist texts even in India. Atisha also visited central Tibet and throughout his travels, he and his disciples made corrections and revisions of the Tibetan translations of Buddhist texts. In the process of giving teachings and making revisions and corrections of already-translated texts in western and central Tibet, Atisha acquired a Tibetan disciple, Dromtonpa, who is credited with establishing the Kadam tradition of Tibetan Buddhism, which Tsongkhapa (1357-1419) transformed into the Gelug school. Atisha passed away in Nyethang in central Tibet and his remains were preserved in a stupa.

Tibet's dismemberment into small principalities and domains during this time allowed the local rulers to finance individual Tibetan scholars to travel to India in search of Buddhist knowledge. This was the case with Drokmi, (992-1072), whose journeys to Nepal and India were financed by the Tibetan ruler of western Tsang. In Vikramashila, Drokmi studied at the feet of Santipa who initiated the Tibetan scholar to various texts, including Hevajra Tantra, which the scholar translated into Tibetan. This text became the basic focus of study of the Sakya school of Tibetan Buddhism which Khon Kunchog Gyalpo, a student of Drokmi, founded.

Another scholar and traveller was Marpa, (1012-1096). He had initially studied at the feet of Drokmi but decided to make his own expeditions to India and Nepal and eventually came across Naropa, with whom, according to one of Marpa's own poems, he stayed sixteen years and seven months. He brought back with him, according to Stein, "the mystical songs (*doha*) of the Tantric poets of Bengal, and the doctrine called Mahamudra, the Great Seal, which he handed over to Milarepa, his chief Tibetan disciple.

The Emergence of the Four Schools of Tibetan Buddhism

These efforts by the Tibetan scholars and translators in making arduous and numerous journeys to receive the teachings enabled the succeeding generations to establish most of the schools of Tibetan Buddhism. These schools and the monasteries they spawned throughout Tibet, in the absence of a central authority, acquired immense prestige and authority and paved the way for Buddhism to acquire political authority. The emergence of the four traditions of Buddhism stabilized Tibetan civilization and made Tibet the centre of learning for High Asia and the Himalayan region.

The Nyingma Tradition

Nyingma is Tibetan Buddhism's oldest school. According to the late Dilgo Khyentse Rinpoche in his introduction to the Nyingma tradition, published in Graham Coleman's *A Handbook of Tibetan Culture*, "The Nyingma tradition has three main streams of transmission: the distant canonical lineage, *kama*; the close lineage of spiritual treasures, *terma*; and the profound pure visions, *dagnang*." Nyingma tradition traces its lineage to the primordial Buddha, Samantabhadra, through Padmasambhava (Guru Rinpoche) and other great masters.

One of the important features of the Nyingma tradition is the *terma*, hidden spiritual treasures. These were hidden by Guru Rinpoche and he predicted his disciples would reincarnate to reveal these treasures for the benefit of all beings. *The Tibetan Book of the Dead* is credited as one such treasure concealed by Guru Rinpoche. Those who find these treasures are called *tertons*, or treasure masters.

This school produced many great spiritual luminaries, including Gyalwa Longchen Rabjampa (1308-1363) who compiled the teachings of Dzogchen, or the great completion, the ultimate teachings of the Tantras on the nature of mind and phenomenon.

The Kagyu Tradition

The Kagyu school traces its lineage to Tilopa, who taught Naropa, who in turn taught Marpa, the great Tibetan translator. Marpa taught Milarepa, the poet-saint of Tibet, and he passed on the entire Kagyu teachings to Gampopa, (1079-1153), his principal disciple. Gampopa passed these teachings to his many disciples and the Kagyu tradition eventually grew into four major and eight minor lineages.

The Kagyu lineage put into practice the concept of reincarnation. When the great Kagyu master Karmapa Dusum Khyenpa (1110-1193), an outstanding disciple of Gampopa, passed away his reincarnation was discovered and duly recognized. Soon other schools adopted this practice of reincarnation.

The Sakya Tradition

In his introduction to the Sakya lineage published in Graham Coleman's *Handbook of Tibetan Culture*, Sakya Trizin, the present throne-holder, explains the origins of his lineage in this way.

"The Sakya Tradition originated in the eleventh century, and has been closely connected with of one of the 'holy families' of Tibet, the Khon family, since early times. One of the family members, Khon Lui Wangpo Sungwa, became a disciple of the great Indian saint Padmasambhava in the eighth century, being amongst the first seven monks to be ordained in Tibet. Through the next thirteen generations, the Khon family was an acknowledged pillar of the 'early propagation' in Tibet. However, it was Khon Konchok Gyalpo who, in 1073, built Sakya monastery and thereby established the foundation of the Sakya Tradition in Tibet. He studied under Drokmi the Translator (992-1072) and soon became a master of many profound teachings. The next centuries saw the rise of the Sakya Tradition to great heights, not only as a pre-eminent spiritual centre but also as a political power in Tibet."

The Gelug Tradition

The Gelug school of Tibetan Buddhism was founded by Tsongkhapa (1357-1419) based on the Kadam tradition of Atisha and his chief Tibetan disciple Dromtonpa. Ganden Tri Rinpoche Yeshe Dhondup, the ninety-ninth throne-holder of Tsongkhapa, in his introduction to the Gelug tradition published in Graham Coleman's *A Handbook of Tibetan Culture*, writes, "Tsongkhapa was particularly attracted by the Kadam's emphasis on the Mahayana principles

19

of universal compassion and altruism, valuing these qualities not only as a spiritual orientation, but more importantly, as a way of life. In this regard, Tsongkhapa saw the study and practice of such Indian classics as the *Bodhisattvacaryavatara* of Shantideva (The Guide to the Boddhisatva's Way of Life) and the *Ratnavali* (Precious Garland) of Nagarjuna as highly supportive to an individual's path to Buddhahood. However, in Tsongkhapa's tradition, the Kadam approach is combined with a strong emphasis on the cultivation of an in-depth insight into the doctrine of emptiness as propounded by Nargarjuna and Chandrakirti."

Tsongkhapa's foremost disciples were Gyaltsab Je (1364-1431), Khedrub Gelek Pelsang (1385-1438) and the first Dalai Lama, Gedun Drub (1391-1474), who established the Tashilhunpo monastery in Shigatse, which remains the spiritual seat of successive Panchen Lamas.

With the establishment of Ganden monastery near Lhasa, Tsongkhapa's principal disciples founded many monastic institutions, which produced extraordinary masters and scholars, generation after generation. The Gelug school's greatest moment came in 1642 when the Great Fifth Dalai Lama assumed political authority of all Tibet.

The Monastic Education System and Its Impact on Tibet

The characteristic of the second spread of Buddhism in Tibet was the profusion of great monasteries. In his book *Tibet: Land of Snow,* Tucci writes, "Shalu, which was to be famous for the great encyclopaedic scholar, Buton, was founded in 1040, Sakya in 1073, Thil in 1158, Drigung in 1179, Tshel in 1175, Tsurphu in 1189."

The emergence of monasteries and monastic institutions throughout Tibet during the second propagation of Buddhism had two lasting consequences. One was that these monasteries contributed to the cultural unity of the Tibetan people. The other was that the monasteries helped the Tibetan people maintain the viability and relevance of the Tibetan Buddhist civilization, generation after generation, down the centuries.

Cementing the Tibetan people together as one culture in a politically truncated and centrally disorganised Tibet were the monasteries. The principal spiritual seats of all the four schools of Tibetan Buddhism were in central Tibet. These seats appointed the abbots and re-confirmed the incarnate lamas of their branch monasteries in far-flung areas throughout the plateau, thus investing central Tibet with high spiritual sanctity. Lhasa became the ultimate destination of pilgrims, which further contributed to the spiritual oneness and cultural homogeneity of the Tibetan people. The fact that by this time Buddhist texts were studied in the common Tibetan script throughout Tibet helped in reinforcing the Tibetan people's cultural unity. In this way, the monasteries served as a centrifugal force that checked Tibet's fissiparous tendencies.

The education system, which these monasteries operated using the Tibetan language as the one and only medium of instruction, contributed to the Tibetan people's linguistic unity. Commentaries on Buddhism made by one scholar of a particular monastery landed up throughout Tibet, being studied and commented on by scholars at the other end of Tibet. For example, *The Hundred Thousand Songs* of Milarepa or the love songs of the sixth Dalai Lama are on the lips of most Tibetans, even to this day. Scholars from all over Tibet and down the centuries, undergoing much trouble, journeyed to central Tibet to complete their higher studies at the principal seats of their tradition. This traffic of ideas and scholars between central Tibet and the frontiers contributed to Tibet's cultural and spiritual wholeness.

The monasteries in Tibet were based on the model of Indian Buddhist universities. These monastic universities taught not only philosophy and logic but also astronomy and medicine, ritual and liturgy, grammar and poetry, even arts and crafts. The Tibetan students and scholars were linguistically equipped to follow the texts and courses. They immersed themselves in this culture and the knowledge it provided. By the 12th century, these Tibetan students and translators had managed to transfer onto Tibetan soil not only the texts, but the whole way of life of Indian Buddhists. This complete importation of Buddhism into Tibetan language made it

21

possible for later Tibetan scholars and masters to study Buddhism and pass it on to their students without any knowledge of Sanskrit or other Indian languages.

Rule by Reincarnation

Karmapa Pakshi was recognised as the reincarnation of the first Karmapa Dusum Khyenpa (1110-1193), an extraordinary disciple of Gampopa. Karmpa Pakshi was the first recognized incarnate lama in Tibetan history. This idea of recognizing reincarnate lamas caught on like fire among the four schools of Tibetan Buddhism. This way of selecting Tibetan spiritual leaders made the leadership succession smooth and by and large provided stable and, in most cases, inspired and inspirational spiritual leadership.

Upon this scene of a spiritually productive and politically crippled Tibet arrived Tsongkhapa, whose followers embraced the idea of reincarnating lamas with unbridled fervour and went on to assume the political authority of a reunited and resurgent Tibet. After the passing away of Gedun Drub, one of Tsongkhapa's three main disciples, the Gelugs recognised Gedun Gyatso as his reincarnation. Both were posthumously recognized as the first and second Dalai Lama. Gedun Gyatso's reincarnation was found in Sonam Gyatso, the third Dalai Lama.

The third Dalai Lama took a step that helped propel the Gelug lineage to assume political authority of all Tibet. He set off from Lhasa in 1577 to visit and preach the Buddhist faith in Mongolia at the invitation of Altan Khan, the chief of the Tumat Mongols. The Mongol Khan converted to Buddhism. In gratitude for the Tibetan lama's spiritual guidance, the Mongol chief conferred on him the title of "Dalai," which means ocean in Mongolian.

In earlier years, Buddhism was a court religion of the Mongol khans both in Mongolia and China. The third Dalai Lama made Buddhism the people's religion in Mongolia. The firm and even irrevocable establishment of the Buddhist faith in Mongolia gave the institution of the Dalai Lama new vigour and an expanding relevance in the

22

tripartite relations, also known as cho-yon, priest-patron relation, among Tibet, Mongolia and China. In their book, *A Cultural History of Tibet*, Snellgrove and Richardson best explain the achievement of the third Dalai Lama. "He travelled not only through those parts of Mongolia which were under the authority of Genghizide khans, but also within the Oirat confederacy, establishing a new 'religious empire' outside Tibet of such size and potential importance that it is not surprising that the Chinese Emperor should be anxious to invite him to Peking."

A child born in 1589 in Mongolia, a son of Chokhur tribal chief, and great-grandson of Altan Khan, was recognised as the fourth Dalai Lama. This fact made the Mongols that much devoted to the institution of the Dalai Lama.

The Tibetan Buddhist civilization reached its apex during the reign of the fifth Dalai Lama, Ngawang Lobsang Gyatso, who, according to Tucci, was "one of Tibet's greatest figures." Because of their devotion to the Dalai Lamas of Tibet, Gushri Khan, the chief of the Qoshot Mongols, and his troops put an end to the long-drawn conflict in central Tibet. In 1642 in Shigatse, Gushri Khan offered the fifth Dalai Lama supreme political and spiritual authority from the borders with Ladakh in the west to Dartsedo (Ch: Tachienlu) in the east along the border of China. Thus began the age of *cho-si zung-drel*, the harmonious blend of religion and politics. The Dalai Lama created the office of the *Desi*, prime minister. He made Lhasa the capital of all Tibet and named his government Ganden Phodrang, the name of his palace in Drepung monastery. He issued laws of public conduct, appointed governors to different districts and a council of ministers to run the new government. A census of the population was conducted for taxation and taxes were collected from all the areas in eastern Tibet.

The prestige of the new government that administered a reunited Tibet attracted attention from Tibet's neighbours. The rulers of Ladakh, Nepal, Sikkim, Bhutan and Shah Suja of Bengal and other kingdoms sent their envoys to pay their respects to the Dalai Lama.

At the same time the Dalai Lama sent a representative and a retinue to advise the various tribes of Mongolia to remain united, instead of engaging in feuds and warfare. Oaths were offered by various Mongol chiefs to this effect to the Dalai Lama through his representative.

The un-stinted devotion of the Mongols to the Dalai Lama revitalized the dynamics of the priest-patron relationship, which during Ming China became defunct. This underlying unity of Mongolia created by the Mongols' devotion to the Dalai Lama prompted the Manchu emperor Shunzhi to dispatch several envoys to Tibet from 1649 to 1651 to invite the Dalai Lama to Beijing. Among other reasons, the looming one for these invitations was to persuade the Dalai Lama to use his spiritual authority with the Mongols to deter them from encroaching upon Manchu China. About the meeting between the lama and emperor, Snellgrove and Richardson write, "Whatever interpretation was placed upon this by the Chinese, it was clearly a meeting between equals. The Emperor himself, in the hope of winning those Mongols who were still hostile but whose devotion to Tibetan Buddhism seemed to be un-diminished, was prepared to disregard the protocol of his new empire and go to the borders of his country to meet the Dalai Lama, while his Chinese advisers even tried to prevent the meeting taking place at all, lest China's authority might be compromised by showing excessive respect for a foreign ruler."

A great new age for Tibet began with the reign of the fifth Dalai Lama. The spiritual connections with Mongolia were strengthened. Just as in the ages past, Tibetan students were eager to learn everything about the Buddhist doctrine and practice from their committed and generous Indian masters, so too were the Mongols keen to study Buddhism from their Tibetan teachers. Mongol students flocked to Tibet to study at the Drepung monastery, the monastery associated personally with the Dalai Lama.

During this period, the Tibetan Buddhist civilization made its way beyond Tibet to Bhutan, Sikkim and the whole northern belt of Nepal. The Tibetan Buddhist civilization had already been well established in Lahaul and Spiti and Ladakh. Along with Mongolia and Kalmykia, Buryatia and Tuva, people from this vast and variegated landmass looked to Tibet as the centre of higher learning and the source of their cultural and spiritual wellspring.

The diffusion of Tibetan Buddhism over this landmass was greatly facilitated when the Tibetans introduced wood block printing technology in Narthang and Lhasa in central Tibet and Derge in Kham. Scriptural texts authored by Tibetan scholars and printed at one of Tibet's three printing presses made their way to the monasteries and temples in every corner of the landmass covered by the Tibetan Buddhist civilization. The production of books and scriptures went on at a furious pace right up to 1959, when the Tibetan people rose up against Chinese communist occupation, which resulted in the flight of His Holiness the 14th Dalai Lama to India, followed by about 80,000 Tibetan refugees.

A Culture without Boundaries

Compared with the changing dynasties in China and India within this span of time, the longevity of the institution of the Dalai Lama is amazing. Throughout its long reign from 1642 when the fifth Dalai Lama assumed political power to 1959 when the 14th Dalai Lama was forced to flee Tibet, the Dalai Lama institution never lost its legitimacy. Unlike China and India, Tibet never faced famines or peasant uprisings that shook or toppled the reigning dynasty.

Tibet now is a culture without a home, a civilization without a country. However, Tibet's cultural attraction to others has never been so deep as today. The fact that it is able to establish itself so well in exile is a credit to the ability of the Tibetan people. It is more of a credit to Buddhist universalism, with its values of compassion and non-violence, incorporated into Tibetan culture. This has attracted and continues to attract the attention, sympathy and admiration of many non-Tibetans who help the Tibetans to study and sustain this culture in many foreign shores and in traditional Tibetan cultural areas outside of Tibet. This has enabled the Tibetans to retain the basic legitimacy and relevance of their culture and the core values of their civilization just as they adjust to the forces of globalization into which they have been thrown.

PART TWO

TIBETOCIDE

Cultural Genocide

"Genocide" comes from Greek *genos* meaning race/tribe and the Latin *cide* meaning killing. Genocide in other words is annihilation of a group. Raphael Lemkin, a Polish law professor who escaped the Nazi occupation of his homeland, first used the term in his book *Axis Rule in Occupied Europe: Laws of Occupation - Analysis of Government - Proposals for Redress* (1944).

Lemkin stated that the term signifies "*a coordinated plan of different actions aiming at the destruction of essential foundations of the life of national groups, with the aim of annihilating the groups themselves. The objectives of such a plan would be disintegration of the political and social institutions, of culture, language, national feelings, religion, and the economic existence of national groups, and the destruction of the personal security, liberty, health, dignity, and even the lives of the individuals belonging to such groups. Genocide is directed against the national group as an entity, and the actions involved are directed against individuals, not in their individual capacity, but as members of the national group.*"

The Convention on the Crime of Genocide, a draft prepared by the Secretary-General of the United Nations in 1947 in pursuance of the resolution of the Economic and Social Council, states that "In this Convention genocide also means any deliberate act committed with intent to destroy the language, religion or culture of a national or racial group on grounds of national or racial origin or religious belief of its members."

According to the UN Declaration on Rights of Indigenous Peoples adopted by the UN General Assembly on 12 September 2007, genocide involves attempts by a more powerful group to dilute the integrity of another group, dispossess them of their lands, assimilate or absorb them into the more powerful culture, or to seek to malign or diminish the minority culture through propaganda. Declaration

27

defines "forced assimilation or the destruction of their culture" as:

a. Any action which has the aim or effect of depriving them of their integrity as distinct peoples, or of their cultural values or ethnic identities;

b. Any action which has the aim or effect of dispossessing them of their lands, territories or resources;

c. Any form of forced population transfer which has the aim or effect of violating or undermining any of their rights;

d. Any form of forced assimilation or integration;

e. Any form of propaganda designed to promote or incite racial or ethnic discrimination directed against them.

An individual right to cultural existence was recognized in the 1948 Universal Declaration of Human Rights and later affirmed in the International Covenant on Economic, Social and Cultural Rights stating that "All peoples have the right of self-determination. By virtue of that right they freely determine their political status and freely pursue their economic, social and cultural development."

However, cultural genocide extends beyond attacks upon the physical and/or biological elements of a group and intends to eliminate its wider institutions. This is done by abolishing a group's language, restrictions on its traditional practices, destruction of religious institutions and objects, the persecution of spiritual teachers, and attacks on cultural figures and intellectuals. Cultural genocide includes suppression of artistic, literary, religious and cultural activities.

The case in point is the International Criminal Tribunal for former Yugoslavia, which held the Serbian destruction of Muslim libraries, mosques and attacks on cultural leaders established genocidal intent against Muslims.

The Chinese government's actions in Tibet go even further with forceful removal of 2.5 million Tibetan nomads from traditional

28

pastoral lives into state-built houses thus destroying over 9000 years of mobile civilization; imposition of language policies which denies the coming generations of Tibetans the right to learn their language, crackdown on Tibetan intellectuals, banning religious festival and restricting cultural activities; the destruction of Tibetan Buddhism by curbing the numbers of monks in monasteries, by subjecting them to intense political campaigns such as 'Patriotic re-education' and by limiting the role of spiritual teachers and forcing the monks into intense ideological studies; and population transfer into Tibet.

Thus Lemkin's original conception of genocide, which expressly recognized that a group could be destroyed by attacking any of these unique aspects, as well as the original UN *ad hoc* Committee on genocide, which defines genocide as "any deliberate act committed with intent to destroy the language, religion or culture of a national or racial group on grounds of national or racial origin or religious belief of its members", applies in the case of Tibet. The Chinese authorities' actions in Tibet may keep the Tibetans biologically intact, but the collective Tibetan identity suffers in a fundamental and irremediable manner.

Destruction Documented by Scholars, Jurists and the UN

If we start from the 7th century, it took the Tibetan people more than 1,300 years to develop and sustain their culture, which, according to Barbara Crossette in her book, *So Close to Heaven: The Vanishing Buddhist Kingdoms of the Himalayas*, "is still one of the world's most appealing civilizations."[1] It took the Chinese Communist Party only about 60 years since its invasion of the country in 1949 to stifle Tibetan culture in its homeland by destroying, among others, the monastic education system that helped the Tibetan people to sustain, refresh and re-energize their culture, century after century.

David Snellgrove and Hugh Richardson explain the reason why they jointly wrote their book, *A Cultural History of Tibet*. "We have taken upon ourselves to write this book at this time because the civilization of the Tibetan people is disappearing before our very eyes, and apart

29

from a few gentle protests here and there the rest of the world lets it go without comment and without regret. Many civilizations have declined and disintegrated in the past, but it is rare that one has the opportunity of being an informed witness of such events."[2]

These two scholars' comment on the Chinese communist destruction in Tibet in the following words: "Since 1959 the Chinese rulers have completely destroyed the main springs of Tibetan civilization. They attacked first the religion and aristocratic social order with a fury unequalled by Cromwell's henchmen in England, and their subsequent devastating onslaughts against the material and religious well-being of ordinary Tibetan farmers, herdsmen and traders may perhaps be compared in methods and results with Cromwell's invasion of Ireland."[3]

The conclusion of these two scholars is supported by the International Commission of Jurists (ICJ), based in Geneva and later by the General Assembly of the United Nations. The International Commission of Jurists (ICJ) published three reports on Tibet. They are *The Question of Tibet and the Rule of Law*, published in 1959, *Tibet and the People's Republic of China: A report to the International Commission of Jurists by its Legal Inquiry Committee on Tibet*, published in 1960, and *Tibet: Human Rights and the Rule of Law*, published in 1997. The conclusion of the first ICJ report is "These inferences were drawn by people who know as no-one outside Tibet can know the full extent of Chinese brutality in Tibet. They are in a better position than any outsider to assess the motives behind the Chinese oppression, including the slaughter, the deportations and the less crude methods, all of which there is abundant evidence. It is therefore the considered view of the International Commission of Jurists that the evidence points to:[4]

" (a) a *prima facie* case of acts contrary to Articles 2 (a) and (e) of the Genocide Convention of 1948;

"(b) a *prima facie* case of a systematic intention by such acts and other acts to destroy in whole or in part the Tibetans as a separate nation and the Buddhist religion of Tibet."

In 1960 ICJ published its second report, *Tibet and the Chinese People's Republic: A Report to the International Commission of Jurists by Its Legal Inquiry Committee on Tibet.* The findings of this report, in the words of the ICJ Secretary-General, "constitute a detailed condemnation of Chinese rule in Tibet."[5] In its third report, ICJ says that the second report "examined the evidence relating to genocide, finding that 'acts of genocide had been committed in an attempt to destroy the Tibetans as a religious group.'"[6]

The ICJ presented its findings on Tibet to the United Nations General Assembly. The UN General Assembly passed a resolution on Tibet in 1959, which called on China to ensure "respect for the fundamental human rights of the Tibetan people and for their distinctive cultural and religious life."[7] In its 1961 General Assembly resolution, the UN called upon China to stop "practices which deprive the Tibetan people of their fundamental human rights and freedoms, including their right to self-determination."[8]

In 1965, the UN General Assembly passed a third resolution, which expressed its grave concern "at the continued violation of the fundamental rights and freedoms of the people of Tibet and the continued suppression of their distinctive cultural and religious life."[9]

As late as 1991, the UN Sub-Commission on Prevention of Discrimination and Protection of Minority Rights passed a resolution in Geneva on 23 August of that year. This resolution expressed its concern "at the continuing reports of violations of fundamental human rights and freedoms which threaten the distinct cultural, religious and national identity of the Tibetan people." It called on China to "fully respect the fundamental human rights and freedoms of the Tibetan people."[10]

The third ICJ report, published in 1997, in the words of its Secretary-General, Adama Dieng, "documents a new escalation of repression in Tibet, characterised by a 're-education' campaign in the monasteries, arrests of leading religious figures and a ban on the public display of photos of the Dalai Lama. It also examines the increasing threats to aspects of Tibetan identity and culture through the transfer of Chinese population into Tibet, the erosion of the Tibetan language and the degradation of Tibet's environment...The report concludes that Tibetans are a 'people under alien subjugation,' entitled to but denied the right of self-determination."[11]

The third ICJ report called "on the United Nations and on nations everywhere to pay heed to the plight of Tibet and to come to the defence of the fundamental principles of international law which have been trampled upon. In particular, the ICJ calls for a referendum to be held in Tibet under United Nations supervision to ascertain the wishes of the Tibetan people."[12]

The third ICJ report found that "repression in Tibet has increased steadily since the 1994 Third National Tibet Work Forum, a key conclave at which senior officials identified the influence of the exiled Dalai Lama, the leading figure in Tibetan Buddhism, as the root of Tibet's instability, and mapped out a new strategy for the region. The Forum endorsed rapid economic development, including the transfer of more Chinese into the Tibet Autonomous Region (TAR), and a campaign to curtail the influence of the Dalai Lama and crackdown on dissent. The results of the Forum included heightened control on religious activity and a denunciation campaign against the Dalai Lama unprecedented since the Cultural Revolution; an increase in political arrests; stepped up surveillance of potential dissidents; and increased repression of even non-political protest."[13]

Tibetan View on the Destruction: the 10th Panchen Lama and His Petition

The views mentioned above are by informed foreign observers of Tibet. However, Tibetans who have lived through the entire experience and who even today still continue to suffer in the country are blunt about the conditions in Tibet. They say Tibet today is a hell on earth and a form of cultural genocide is going on in Tibet. They say the country is still under martial law in everything but in name.

No Tibetan critique of the nature of Chinese rule in Tibet can match that of the late 10th Panchen Lama's in depth, breadth and meticulous detail. Known as the 70,000 character petition, it was addressed to the top Chinese leadership, including Mao Zedong. In his capacity as the vice-chairman of the National People's Congress, in 1962, the Panchen Lama travelled extensively throughout Tibet and wrote his observations of the conditions of the people and places he visited. With the help of the United Front, he set up a team to write the petition. When completed, after much cross-checking and having the petition translated from the original Tibetan into Chinese, the Panchen Lama presented his opinion to the Chinese premier Zhou Enlai on 18 May 1962. The Chinese premier took the criticism in the document seriously to the extent that he summoned Zhang Guohua and Zhang Jingwu, the two top Chinese leaders in Tibet, to Beijing and told them to address the mistakes in their Tibet work.

However, that summer at the central committee conclave at the seaside resort of Beidahe, Mao Zedong called the Panchen Lama's 70,000 character petition "a poisoned arrow" and labelled the Tibetan leader as "a class enemy." The Panchen Lama was struggled or publicly criticised and humiliated before thousands of angry crowds. He was thrown in prison and served 14 years under some form of detention.

Though the Panchen Lama's critique of the nature of Chinese rule in Tibet was made in 1962, more than 55 years ago, it remains valid today, mainly because the Chinese authorities, despite a tentative foray into liberalisation in Tibet, have largely refused to address the core concerns raised by the Tibetan leader. As such this critique remains as relevant today as it was for the Tibetan people more than 55 years ago. The bulk of Tibetan criticism, both within and outside Tibet, against Chinese rule in Tibet echoes the Panchen Lama's petition. But his petition, first of its kind still remains the most detailed, comprehensive and on the spot investigation of China's rule in Tibet that continues to devastate the way of life of the Tibetan people.

The Panchen Lama's 70,000 character petition remained a top secret document for many years. In 1996 a sealed envelope was delivered to the office of the Tibet Information Network (TIN), a London-based news agency focused on Tibet. The envelope contained a Chinese translation of the petition. TIN had the petition translated into English and in 1997 published the document as *A Poisoned Arrow: The Secret Report of the 10th Panchen Lama.*

The Panchen Lama based his critique on the nature of the Chinese rule in Tibet on the assaults made by the party on Tibetan Buddhism, culture, language and the ethnic identity of the Tibetan people. These assaults were made worse by the unfair and arbitrary land distribution, erroneous practices introduced in the new methods of agriculture and animal husbandry, and arbitrary arrests which swelled the prison population in the case of the Tibet Autonomous Region to more than 10% of the region's total human population. All of this, the Panchen Lama wrote, amounted to "taking medicine for one's head for a foot ailment."

In saying this, the Panchen Lama, one of Tibet's highest lamas and China's closest Tibetan ally, fell one breath short of accusing China of deliberate and systematic genocide of the Tibetan people. The case he constructed included the excesses in the suppression of the 1959 uprising, the thousands who were arrested on the mere suspicion of being involved in the Tibetan resistance movement, the rude prison conditions and the inhuman treatment of prisoners, and the famine that followed the introduction of the commune system in all Tibetan areas.

On page 102 of *A Poisoned Arrow*, the Panchen Lama wrote, "We have no way of knowing in detail the number of prisoners who were arrested after the rebellion, but from appearance of things it may be inferred that the number of people who were locked up reached about ten thousand or more than ten thousand in every area (diqu). Therefore, if we say that all these people were the enemy, then we can affirm that hardly anyone is left over amongst us Tibetans, apart from women, old people, children and a very small number of young men. Now, if we say that there are both enemies and those dear to

34

us among those who were locked up, that is even more absurd. To arrest and lock up all people without distinguishing between good and bad contravenes every just law in the world."

On page 36 of *A Poisoned Arrow*, the Panchen Lama made these comments on the treatment of the prisoners. "In addition, the guards and cadres threatened prisoners with cruel, ruthless and malicious words and beat them fiercely and unscrupulously. Also, prisoners were deliberately transferred back and forth, from the plateau to the lowlands, from freezing cold to very warm, from north to south, up and down, so that they could not accustom themselves to their new environment. Their clothes and quilts could not keep their bodies warm, their mattresses could not keep out the damp, their tents and buildings could not shelter them from the wind and rain and the food could not fill their stomachs. Their lives were miserable and full of deprivation, they had to get up early for work and come back late from their work; what is more, these people were given the heaviest and most difficult work, which inevitably led to their strength declining from day to day. They caught many diseases, and in addition they did not have sufficient rest; medical treatment was poor, which caused many prisoners to die from abnormal causes. All prisoners in their fifties and sixties, who were physically weak and already close to death, were also forced to carry out heavy and difficult physical labour. When I went back and forth on my travels and saw such scenes of suffering, I could not stop myself from feeling grief and thinking with a compassionate heart 'Why can't things be different?'"

On the advice of his senior attendants, tutors and colleagues, the Panchen Lama held back from his petition many of the more gruesome findings he saw during his travels in Tibet in 1962. Later, after his release and rehabilitation, in the more relaxed political environment that prevailed in China he made the following comments in his address to the TAR Standing Committee of the National People's Congress held in Beijing in March 1987. This address was smuggled out of Tibet, transcribed and translated into English by the Department of Information and International Relations of the Central Tibetan Administration and first published in 1998 and reprinted in 2003 as *From the Heart of the Panchen Lama*. On page 66 of this booklet, the Panchen Lama used stronger language to describe China's past mistakes in Tibet. He said, "In Qinghai, for example, there are between three to four thousand villages and towns, each having between three to four thousand families with four to five thousand people. From each town and village, about 800 to 1000 people were imprisoned. Out of this, at least three hundred to four hundred people died in prison. This means almost half of the prison population perished. Last year (1986), we discovered that only a handful of people had participated in the rebellion. Most of these people were completely innocent. In my 70,000 character petition, I have mentioned that about 5 percent of the population had been imprisoned. According to my information at that time, it was between 10 to 15 percent. But I did not have the courage to state such a huge figure. I would have died under *thamzing* if I had stated the real figure."

In the address, the Panchen Lama recounted an incident from the 1960s. "There was one woman, a wife of one of my staff, who was also arrested. One day, when she was called into the interrogation chamber, she muttered, 'this man called Panchen had caused me so much suffering that I will die of depression.' This utterance led the authorities into believing that she would say something incriminating about me, a much-awaited chance for the authorities to take punitive measures against me. They immediately called the scribes to record her testimony. Then she went on, 'We made a big mistake by following this man called Panchen and not participating in the fight against the Chinese. If he had led us in rebellion against the Chinese, our condition today would be better than this. Because, initially, we would have killed as many Chinese as possible and then fled to India, which would have been easy since India is near our village. But this man told us to be progressive and patriotic. And this is what we get for following his advice. Now it is not possible for us to flee to India. Our people, both men and women, are being persecuted here. We are experiencing hell on earth."

In the same address, the Panchen Lama said, "If there was a film made on all the atrocities perpetrated in Qinghai province, it would shock the viewers. In Golok area, many people were killed and their dead bodies rolled down the hill into a big ditch. The soldiers told the family members and relatives of the dead people that they should all celebrate since the rebels had been wiped out. They were even forced to dance on the dead bodies. Soon after, the family members and relatives were also machine-gunned. They were all buried there."

One topic the Panchen Lama returned to frequently in his petition was the famine which swept Tibet and the starvation that followed. His petition is replete with accounts of Tibetans, lacking grains and meat, being forced to eat tree barks, grass and grain husks. Starvation swept Tibet. In some places, the Panchen Lama said the spectre of whole families starving to death was a common experience.

On page 29 of *A Poisoned Arrow*, the Panchen Lama wrote, "Consequently, in some places in Tibet, a situation arose where people starved to death. This really should not have happened. It was an awful business and very serious. In the past, although Tibet was a society ruled by dark and savage feudalism, there had never been such a shortage of grain. In particular, because Buddhism was widespread, all people, whether noble or humble, had the good habit of giving help to the poor, and so people could live solely by begging for food. A situation could not have arisen where people starved to death, and we have never heard of a situation where people starved to death."

However, Tibet was not alone to suffer from the twin curse of famine and starvation. The whole of China was blighted. Chairman Mao's the Great Leap Forward, and herding more than 90 percent of the entire population of China into communes was the direct cause of the famine that lasted from 1958 to 1962, which, according to some scholars, claimed at least 20 million lives. Others say about 40 millions died in the great famine.

But before the great famine was the great confusion, precipitated by

37

the introduction of collectives and communes. On page 106 of his book, *Hungry Ghosts: China Secret Famine*, Jasper Becker recounts the great confusion. "The Party Secretary of Paoma town announced in October 1958 that Socialism would end on November 7 and Communism would begin on November 8. After the meeting, everyone immediately took to the streets and began grabbing goods out of the shops. When the shelves were bare, they went to other people's homes and took their chickens and vegetables home to eat. People even stopped making a distinction as to which children belonged to whom. Only wives were safe from this sharing because the Party secretary was unsure about this. So he asked the higher-level authorities for instructions on whether people should continue to be allowed to keep their own wives."

But in all fairness the famine in Tibet, though unprecedented and unheard of in Tibetan history, was relatively mild. The one in China decimated the country. On page 545 of his book, *Why the West Rules – For Now*, Ian Morris recounts this story. "The worst thing that happened during the famine was this: parents would decide to allow the old and the young to die first... A mother would say to her daughter, 'You have to go and see your granny in heaven.' They stopped giving the girl-children food. They just gave them water..."

But more than the loss caused by the famine in Tibet, the Panchen Lama was most concerned about the fate of Tibetan culture, identity and language and Tibetan Buddhism. The Tibetan people can recover from the loss in their ranks. However, the Panchen Lama argued in his petition that if Tibetan identity, language and Tibetan Buddhism and culture were lost, they would be lost forever.

On the fate of Buddhism, the Panchen Lama wrote the following anguished comments. "But what if you took a very lovable, much in demand, vigorous and innocent youth and deliberately put them to death? In just the same way, this is the reason why we, all the people of Tibet, feel that it is unendurable that Buddhism has suffered such a huge decline that it is near extinction."

The Panchen Lama was profoundly pessimistic about the future of Tibetan Buddhism under China's authoritarian rule. In the petition he said, "As for the future without religion, in Tibetan areas in brother provinces, after suppression of the rebellion, owing to various types of direct and indirect obstructions by lower level Party and government cadres, even the names of the activities of 'teaching, debating, writing' of Buddhist scriptures, which were as vast as the ocean, are no longer heard; needless to say, even the name of religious culture can be seen to be disappearing. Under these actual circumstances, the future of religion has in reality been destroyed; therefore, in fact, religion has no future."

What if the top Chinese leadership had listened to the Panchen Lama's pointed criticism and implemented his suggestions? Would China have avoided the catastrophe of the Cultural Revolution which nearly tore the country apart? Could this have made China jump-start its resurgence more than two decades before Deng Xiaoping's reform and opening up of the late 1970s?

The tragedy of the Panchen Lama and perhaps for China and certainly for Tibet was that his criticism of the nature of Chinese rule in Tibet was made at a time when an intense power struggle was developing within the topmost ranks of the party. It was a time when Mao decided to smash the party to re-orient China to his vision of a permanent revolution. Any criticism of party policy towards the minorities was considered criticism flung at Mao and his leadership. In this way, a view expressed by one of the highest Tibetan lamas and whose loyalty to China was beyond question on what was wrong with China's Tibet policy was swallowed in the drum beat of war Mao launched on his party and in the chaos and confusion of the Cultural Revolution. The Cultural Revolution resulted in, according to Henry Kissinger, a faithful friend of China, "spectacular human and institutional carnage, as one by one, China's organs of power and authority – including the highest ranks of the Communist Party – succumbed to the assaults of teenage ideological shock troops."

But the Tibetan leader wasn't done as yet. During 14 years of his disappearance, many in Tibet did not know whether he was alive or dead. This doubt was cleared away when on 26 February 1978, Xinhua announced his presence at the 5ᵗʰ National Committee of the Chinese People's Political Consultative Conference in Beijing. In 1980, the Panchen Lama was reinstated as Vice-Chairman of the National People's Congress. The Panchen Lama's political rehabilitation was complete.

The years of public humiliation, solitary confinement and overall suffering inflicted on him had not dimmed his trenchant views of China's Tibet policy or sapped his energy and courage of conviction. Given the new relative freedom and his old official posts restored to him, the Panchen Lama bounced back in the political fray as never before. Speaking to a gathering of Tibetans during the Monlam Festival (the Great Prayer Festival) in Lhasa in 1985, the Panchen Lama said, "His Holiness the Dalai Lama and I are spiritual friends. There are no difference between His Holiness the Dalai Lama and me. Some people are trying to create discord between us. This will not succeed."

At the TAR Standing Committee of the National People's Congress, held in Beijing in March 1987, the Panchen Lama openly criticised the Chinese government's policy in Tibet regarding education, economic development, population transfer and discriminatory treatment of Tibetans.

On 9 January 1989 the Panchen Lama arrived in Shigatse, Tibet's second largest town and the traditional fief and parish of Tibet's Panchen Lamas, to consecrate the newly-renovated mausoleums of the Fifth through the Ninth Panchen Lamas at his main monastery of Tashi Lhunpo. On 24 January in his address to the monks of Tashi Lhunpo and the people of Shigatse, the Panchen Lama said that the Chinese rule in Tibet had brought more destruction than benefit to the Tibetan people.

The Panchen Lama survived his 70,000 character petition. But this his last judgment of Chinese rule in Tibet cost the Panchen Lama his life. On 28 January, four days after delivering this blistering and historic condemnation of Chinese rule, the Panchen Lama was found dead at his monastery. His death followed the drama of two Panchen Lamas. But that is another story told in riveting detail by Isabel Hilton in her *The Search for the Panchen Lama*.

However, the Panchen Lama's critique of the nature of Chinese rule in Tibet both in his 1962 petition and after his release from prison forms the intellectual framework of Tibet's essential argument against China. The issues the Panchen Lama raised with growing vehemence and alarm have become the core concerns of the Tibetan people in Tibet and elsewhere. These issues of core concern to the Tibetan people cover the destruction of the spiritual institutions that maintained the vitality of Tibetan Buddhism in Tibet, the unremitting assault on Tibetan culture, the growing marginalisation of the Tibetan language, China's population transfer policy which is reducing Tibetans to a minority in their own land and the degradation of Tibet's environment in the name of development which essentially is aimed at attracting more Chinese settlers onto the plateau. To these arguments, China still does not provide either convincing answers or effective policy remedies.

Since the Panchen Lama's death, voices within Tibet and the Chinese communist establishment that call on China to change its hard line Tibet policy are growing in both volume and urgency. One critically important voice is that of the late Phuntsok Wangyal's, or Phunwang as he is popularly known, an insiders' insider of a Tibetan within the Chinese communist establishment. But he was one of the towering figures in modern Tibetan history and in Tibet's interface with a revolutionary, resurgent and unified communist China. He founded the Tibetan Communist Party whose aim was to reform Tibet's outdated political and social structure under a re-unified administration of the three provinces of central, eastern and north-eastern Tibet. He took his plea for reforming Tibet's political system to some of the progressive officials within Tibet's ruling aristocracy. To one of them, Yuthok Tashi Thondup, the governor-general of eastern Tibet based in Chamdo, Phunwang said, "The world is changing very quickly. I think if we do not reform ourselves, we will destroy ourselves. We won't have to worry about the Chinese or anyone else. We will be our worst enemy." These thoughts are recounted in his fascinating autobiography as told to Melvyn Goldstein in *A Tibetan Revolutionary: The Political Life and Times of Bapa Phuntso Wangye*. Though he received a sympathetic hearing from Tibetan aristocrats like Yuthok, the Tibetan government in Lhasa brushed off Phunwang's ideas of the need for political and social reform. In the end, Phunwang merged his Tibetan Communist Party with the Chinese Communist Party and on 9 September 1951 led the advanced troops of the People's Liberation Army into Lhasa.

But even this devoted son of the Chinese communist revolution, whose vital contributions to China's "liberation" of Tibet were acknowledged by the likes of Mao Zedong and Deng Xiaoping, was not spared the xenophobic wrath of the Chinese communists. In 1958 he came under suspicion for advocating Tibetan independence. He was bundled off to prison where he remained for nearly 20 years. In 1978 he was released and rehabilitated. Like the late Panchen Lama, the late Phunwang continued to advocate equality between the Tibetans and the majority Chinese. In his three letters sent to Chinese President Hu Jintao, the veteran Tibetan revolutionary urged the Chinese leadership to resolve the issue of Tibet with the Dalai Lama based on the Tibetan leader's idea of the Middle-Way Approach of Tibet enjoying total internal autonomy within the scope of the Chinese constitution.

In his letter of 29 October 2004 addressed to President Hu Jintao, Phunwang said, "Comrade Hu Jintao, you were the leader of Tibet, you understand Tibet, the feelings and hearts of the common Tibetans, you are aware of the facts about the Tibet issue. Today, once the Tibet issue is satisfactorily solved, you and the central party leaders can meet the Dalai Lama with affection in the capital of the People's Republic of China, which will make a stir in the whole world and in China – especially in every corner of the Land of Snow, there will be great rejoicing."

In the same letter to President Hu Jintao, Phunwang said, "Life experience shows us that an excessive emphasis being placed on one side will mask the extreme partiality of the other side. In light of the political phenomenon that 'stability overrides all', the horrible words 'Free Tibet' have become a 'phobia' to some people for whom even 'Tibetans demanding to study the Tibetan language, to use the Tibetan language, would lead to Tibetan independence activities'. On the other side, the words have become a 'money-earning tree' for some departments to keep on asking for funds from the Central Government, thereby setting an example for some autonomous prefectures in inland China of how to develop the knack for making money. There is even such a saying: 'Inner Mongolia is asking for money, they are denied; Xinjiang is asking for money, sometimes they are given; Tibet is not asking money, they are given'."

Blaming China's hard line policy on Tibet on the vast anti-splittism bureaucracy, he said, "There is also another saying: 'These people live on anti-separatism, are promoted due to anti-separatism, and they hit the jackpot by anti-separatism'. To summarise the sayings above: 'The longer the Dalai Lama keeps on staying abroad, and the bigger his influence, the more long-lasting the period of high ranks and great wealth for those anti-separatism groups; on the contrary, when the Dalai Lama restores relations with the Central Government, these people will be terrified, tense and lose their jobs'."

His legacy of having worked for the Chinese establishment in Tibet made Phunwang hold back many of his punches. But those who are not so constrained are much more critical of the nature of Chinese rule in Tibet. In his book *The Line Between Sky and Earth*, Shogdung, then 47-year-old editor at the Qinghai Nationalities Publishing House in Xining in Northeastern Tibet, who was arrested on 23 April 2010, writes that after the overwhelmingly peaceful protests in Tibet in 2008, the Chinese authorities have heavily cracked down and used their guns on unarmed Tibetans "hunting them down like innocent wild animals, like pigs, yaks and sheep killed in slaughter-house and scattered them like a heap of peas" and turned Tibet into "a 21st century place of terror."[1]

Similarly in his book *The Fierce Courage* by Gartse Jigme, the author living in Tibet whose grandfather died of starvation during Mao's Great Leap Forward campaign, writes about the arrest of Jigme, a monk from Labrang monastery in northeastern Tibet in 2008. Gartse Jigme writes that the monk was handcuffed, shackled and was tied to a chair with a black cloth covering his face. One of the four Chinese soldiers while pressing his gun over the monk's head said, "This gun was made to kill Tibetans, especially the monks. If I kill and dump your body in a gutter no one will even find out!"[2] Gartse Jigme further writes that "the psychological pain from crackdowns and the sufferings that Tibetans are forced to undergo are unbearable."[3]

Arjia Rinpoche, the abbot of Kumbum Monastery and a survivor of 'reform through hard labour' campaign, who later held many important posts in the Chinese Buddhist Association, fled China in the late 1990s. In his memoir *Surviving the Dragon: A Tibetan Lama's Account of 40 Years Under Chinese Rule* published in 2010, Arjia Rinpoche says, "Modern Chinese history can be characterized as a 'Tail of Three Fish.' Taiwan is still swimming in the ocean. No one has caught that fish – at least not yet. Hong Kong is alive but on display in a Chinese aquarium. Tibet, the third fish, is broiled and on the table, already half devoured: its language, its religion, its culture and its native people are disappearing faster than its glacial ice."[4]

The conditions in Tibet today are getting worse, though the situation in the past was no less difficult. Tibet experienced its first famine in its recorded history in the late 1950s and early 1960s. In their testimonies, Lama Karma Tenzin and seven other Tibetans who came into exile in 1969 and 1970, write in *Tibet Under Chinese Communist Rule: A Compilation of Refugee Statements 1958-1975* that in Zurmong, a small town in eastern Tibet, "...all young men had died either in battles or of starvation. The women and children were hedged together to work in the communes and all goods and animals were collectivised. Only a few old men were left in town. The workers were given only one spoonful of *tsampa* each day which they had to supplement with wild plants and the flesh of dead horses and goats."[5]

They further state that "the produce of the commune, grains, meat, butter, etc. are mostly siphoned off to meet the needs of the 'State Grain Reserve', 'War Preparation Reserve', etc. and only a small fraction is left for consumption by commune members."[6]

In the same book, Yeshi Choephel, who came into exile in 1970, says that "most of the produce was collected as 'Patriotic Grain Tax' and taken away without compensation. The remaining harvest is 'purchased' at a nominal price which is again never paid ... Since then many died of starvation, some hanged themselves and some jumped into rivers."[7]

Dr Lobsang Wangyal, the former personal physician to His Holiness the Dalai Lama and a survivor of the Chinese gulag, writes in his autobiography *My Land My Culture* that "Each day six to ten prisoners died of starvation. The surrounding areas of Samye were full of buried corpses and, when a strong wind blew, the sand got blown away and dead bodies became exposed...Lack of food and hunger drove us to pick up the smallest insects that crawled on the earth. Carcasses of dead horses, donkeys, dogs and rats became novelties for us. I saw many prisoners dig in toilets in search of insects. A father and son from Gyangtse collected insects in a tin can as we dug canals and ate them in the evenings after boiling them. Many were too exhausted to do anything; they just sat in the toilet and ate the worms that came from their excrement."[8]

In his book *Nagtsang Zhilui Kyiduk* or *Suffering of Nagtsang Boy*, Nuden Lodoe, who was 10-years-old in 1958, writes: "In the three communes of Dekyiling [a small village in north-eastern Tibet], there were about a thousand children and about six hundred elder people...now there are only about 50 children and ten elderly people in the three communes. Rest all died in about six months. In fact, they all died in about a couple of months."[9]

Tibetans record that 1.2 million Tibetans died since the early 1950's to 1984 through starvation, in the fighting, in prison, by torture and execution, and because of suicide. A confidential official Chinese

45

document *Tibet's Status and Basic Duties and Education* published by the TAR Military's Political Bureau in October 1960 states that "from March 1959 [to 1960] 87,000 enemies were exterminated."[10] Another official document *Tibet's Rebellion Quelled* published by TAR People's Publishing House states that from 29 February to 15 April 1960, over 18,000-strong PLA soldiers surrounded the 'rebellions' and "killed 1100, injured 4800, arrested more than 4100 and exterminated all the enemies in these areas[11] [Tengchen, Lhari Dzong, Ngamda and Shopamdo]"

Likewise, in 1956 Golok in eastern Tibet had over 140,000 people, "but by 1964 census, their numbers had dropped to 70,000."[12] Most died during the famine caused by the Great Leap Forward (1958-1961) and others killed by the occupying Chinese forces. In his book *In Exile from the Land of Snow*, John Avedon writes "according to one survivor who spent twenty-one years in five separate [labour] camps, roughly 70,000 Tibetan were imprisoned in north of Lanzhou, 35,000 of whom perished from starvation in 1959-61."[13]

Arjia Rinpoche was forced to undergo 16 years of forced labour. In 1998, unable to "stand the dishonesty that was being forced (on him) to experience on a daily basis,"[14] he came into exile. In *Surviving the Dragon* he writes that Yang Qing Xi, a veteran Chinese cadre, told him about an incident in 1958. "One night the cadres of the People's Liberation Army called the villagers [Gomang County in Amdo] to a meeting held in a local barn. After about 20 minutes, they announced that they had to execute all counterrevolutionaries and rebels. The cadres left the building, locking the door behind them, and then tossed grenades into the barn. The military had already surrounded the area, prepared to shoot anyone who tried to escape. About 200 people, including women, children, and elders, perished…their corpses were tossed into the fields where dogs and wild animals set upon them. The next year, when farmers planted their crops, they found arms and legs scattered everywhere."

The physical destruction was equally immense. In the early 1980's, of the reported 6,000 monasteries and temples throughout Tibet, only 13 were standing intact. The rest were razed to the ground, their treasures and invaluable statues and religious artefacts looted and carted away to China. Many of them found their way in the art markets of Hong Kong and Tokyo. These monasteries were centres of higher learning. Their complete obliteration means that the institutions and tradition that continuously produced outstanding scholars, practitioners and masters who enriched Tibetan culture and the lives of millions of non-Tibetans came to an end within the homeland. This situation is like India or America waking up one fine day to discover that all their universities and institutions of higher learning and the members of the faculty and student population have vanished overnight.

All these are taking place in Tibet today. Under Den Xiaoping's liberalization, Tibet enjoyed a brief spell of relaxed policy as Hu Yaobang took charge as China's party chief. Hu visited Tibet in May 1980 and at a major conference of cadres, both Tibetan and Chinese, Hu blasted them for their failure to improve the livelihood of the Tibetan people. He said the Chinese Communist Party had let down the Tibetans. In some areas, he said, the livelihood of the Tibetan people had deteriorated below the pre-1959 level.

Hu Yaobang said, "Our present situation is less than wonderful because the Tibetan people's lives have not been much improved. There are some improvements in some parts, but in general, Tibetans still live in relative poverty. In some areas the living standards have even gone down. We comrades in the Central Committee, Chairman Hua, as well as several vice-chairmen, were very upset when we heard about this situation. We feel very bad! The sole purpose of our communist party is to work for the happiness of the people, to do good things for them. We have worked nearly thirty years, but the life of the Tibetan people has not been notably improved. Are we not to blame? If we don't make this clear, people won't let us off the hook; party members won't let us get away with it."[15]

He then outlined a six-point plan that was to allow Tibet to exercise full regional autonomy, Tibetans would be exempted from taxes for a period of three years, a liberal economic policy suited to Tibet's special characteristics would be adopted, more of Tibet's share of the state subsidy would be pumped into agriculture and animal husbandry, Tibetan culture, language and education would be improved and the party's policy on minority cadres would be implemented. There was also the talk that about 85% of the Chinese cadres based in Tibet would be withdrawn in phases.

These measures allowed Tibet partly to recover culturally and economically. Destroyed monasteries were allowed to be re-built and those damaged repaired. Tibet opened to tourism, which strengthened the economy. The Tibetan people's religious life re-surfaced, which added to the attraction of international tourists. This period of liberalization allowed Tibet to partially recover from the earlier devastation.

However, this liberalization was shorted-lived. Hu was toppled from power in 1987. One reason for getting rid of him was his liberal Tibet policy. That year Lhasa was rocked by protests. The authorities retaliated by arrests and imprisonment. Bigger and more sustained protests shook Lhasa in 1988 and 1989.[16] Hu Jintao, the former Chinese president, then the party boss in Tibet, imposed martial law in 1989, the first martial law in the country since the founding of the People's Republic of China. It lasted more than a year. In the same year the Panchen Lama suddenly died amid deep suspicion and misgiving. But these protests were dwarfed by the Chinese students' mass protest at the Tiananmen Square that shook China. Zhao Ziyang, the liberal prime minister who advocated reconciliation and dialogue with the students, was put under house arrest and the conservatives in the leadership closed ranks and militarily crushed the student movement.

These events boded ill for Tibet. With the conservatives in charge, the leadership's attitude and policy to Tibet changed dramatically. This is reflected in the tone and shift of emphasis in the policy directive that came out of the Third Tibet Work Forum held in 1994. A policy known as "grasping with both hands"[17] was announced, which pushed for rapid economic development for Tibet while coming down hard and mercilessly on Tibetan nationalists. Tibetan separatism was considered the major cause of instability in Tibet and a campaign was carried out to extirpate Tibetan nationalism. A denunciation campaign was launched against the Dalai Lama to root out his influence. Thus began the subtle but equally damaging second Cultural Revolution against the core values of the Tibetan people, which Tibetans consider as cultural genocide.

Why the Destruction?

The reason for this destruction is not found in the Chinese people, who repeatedly proved themselves and their culture to be cosmopolitan, inclusive and embracing. Note the tolerance shown, down the centuries, to Buddhism, Christianity, Islam and other non-Chinese faiths. Confucian China might have exhibited a degree of condescension, but not intolerance, to the non-Chinese world, dismissing many in the imperial periphery as "barbarians,"[1] from whom the Middle Kingdom had nothing to learn but had much to teach in the ways of developing and operating a civilized society. Though China was dismissive of the cultural development of the peoples who operated outside its imperial fringes, there was one and the only one country to which China sent students to learn and invited masters to teach. That country was India. That was because of Buddhism, the spiritual tradition that had established itself in India, and which fanned out from the country and embedded itself as the core value of many cultural and national identities in large parts of Asia, including China.

China's admiration for Buddhism is best expressed by Xuanzang, the 7th century Chinese traveller to India who spent many years in Nalanda studying Buddhism and other related subjects. His journey to India along the Silk Road is immortalised in the Chinese epic, *Journey to the West*. In response to the pleas of the teachers and students of Nalanda not to return to China, Xuanzang, as quoted in Amartya Sen's *The Argumentative Indian: Writings on Indian Culture, History and Identity*, responded by saying, "Buddha established his

49

doctrine so that it might be diffused to all lands. Who would wish to enjoy it alone and forget those who are not yet enlightened?"[2]

The spread of Buddhism to China made a major contribution to correcting Chinese self-centredness and opening Chinese mind to a higher and wider appreciation of cultures and wisdom emanating from other realms. This means that Buddhist Tibet's destruction at the hands of communist China does not lie in either the Chinese people or their culture. It lies in the intolerance China imported in the form of communism from the West. More specifically, it lies in the Leninist state structure in China that considers Tibetan culture and identity as a fundamental challenge to the party's rule in Tibet.

Chinese Communist Leaders' View of Tibetan Culture: "Religion is Poison"

During his final meeting with the Dalai Lama in 1954, Mao Zedong edged closer to the Tibetan leader and whispered: "... but of course religion is poison. It has two great defects: it undermines the race, and secondly it retards the progress of the country. Tibet and Mongolia have been both poisoned by it."[1]

Four decades later, in his speech at the 1993 Working Meeting of the United Work Front Department, Jiang Zemin, the then President of China said, "[We are] asking them [monastic community] to love the motherland, to support the socialist system and the leadership of the Communist Party. We don't allow religion to be used to confront the leadership of the Party and the socialist system."[2]

Later, Mao's animosity to Buddhism and Jiang's demands re-surfaced as China's official policy. Beijing held the Third Work Forum on Tibet in 1994, which recommended putting an end "to the unbridled construction of monasteries and nunneries as well as to the unbridled recruitment of monks/nuns."[3] The forum further advocated that "the struggle between ourselves and the Dalai Clique is neither a matter of religious belief, nor a matter of question of autonomy, it is a matter of securing unity of our country and opposing splittism... This is a life-and-death struggle."[4]

The forum initiated a campaign of 'striking relentless blows' against 'the Dalai clique' and 'separatists' as one of the "important elements" of the comprehensive management of public security.

Jiang Zemin, who presided over the forum, said that " it is necessary [for Tibetan culture] to absorb the fine cultures of other nationalities in order to integrate the fine traditional culture with the fruits of modern culture. This will facilitate the development of a socialist new culture in Tibet."[5]

On 14 May 1996, Chen Kuiyuan, who in January 1992 succeeded Hu Jintao as the party secretary of TAR said, "There are a few die-hard reactionaries in the monasteries who are hell-bent on following the Dalai,"[6] and that "In order to beat the splittists and sabotage activities of the Dalai Clique and protect the normal religious life of the masses of religious devotees, we must carry out a carefully differentiated rectification of the monasteries within our region."[7]

On 23 July 1996, Chen launched the so-called spiritual civilization campaign and declared its main thrust in Tibet. He said, "One of the most important tasks in facilitating the spiritual civilization drive is to screen and eliminate Dalai's influence in the spiritual field. If we fail to accomplish this task, we cannot claim to have attained any great results in facilitating the spiritual campaign drive."

On 14 May 1996 in a speech to the Party Section Meeting in Tibet, Chen said, "Communists are atheist. If we see the Dalai as a religious ideal and avoid denouncing him in the process of the anti-splittist campaign, then politically we will not be able to lead the masses to fight effectively against the splittist group headed by him. We must denounce him fundamentally and not recognise his religious authority."[8]

On 8 November 1997, in a speech to the "TAR" Party Committee, Chen said, "Religious believers, and even some Party members and cadres, are not able to free themselves from the shackles of their outlook on the world as seen from the religious idealism.... They waste their precious time in futile efforts in praying for individual

51

happiness in the next world; instead of using their limited financial resources to improve their economic condition, they unrestrictedly donate their money to monasteries; instead of letting their children receive a modern education, they send them to monasteries to become a monk or a nun. Such negative thinking and behaviour prevents science and technology from spreading..."[9]

In 1997, Li Ruihuan, a Politburo member said, "Expanding Tibet's economy is not a mere economic issue, but a major political issue that has a vital bearing on Tibet's social stability and progress. This work not only helps Tibet, but is also related directly to the struggle against the Dalai Lama's splittist attempts."

In 1998 during a televised dialogue with the then US President Bill Clinton during his China visit, Jiang Zemin said, "Last year when I visited the USA and also some European countries, I found that many well-educated people actually believed in the doctrines of Lamaism. I think this is a problem which needs to be studied. Why? Why?"[10]

In his March 1999 speech to ethnic and religious leaders at the Ninth Chinese People's Political Consultative Conference, Jiang Zemin announced, "To correctly handle religious problems, first we should completely and correctly implement the party's religious policy; second, we should strengthen management of religious affairs according to the law; third, we should actively guide religions to adapt to the socialist society."[11]

On 19 July 2001, in a speech at the rally in celebration of the 50th 'peaceful liberation' of Tibet, the then Vice-President Hu Jintao said, "The PLA Garrison, PAPF units and the law enforcement departments in Tibet are the strong pillars and loyal guards in defending the frontier of the motherland and maintaining stability in Tibet. They are an important force in building of both material and spiritual civilization,"[12] and that China "ushered in a new era in which Tibet would turn from darkness to light, from backwardness to progress, from poverty to affluence and from seclusion to openness."[13]

The impact of these kinds of intolerance, arrogance and chauvinism of the Chinese leaders on Tibetan culture has been devastating for Tibet. Tibet suffered under policies such as 'democratic reform' and 'patriotic re-education' campaigns that Beijing initiated in Tibet, and the Great Leap Forward, anti-rightist campaign and the Cultural Revolution that Beijing launched throughout China to enforce its ultra-leftist policies.

These campaigns are carried out by a vast bureaucracy entrenched in the party, military and government. It includes social apparatus controls such as 'democratic management committee' in the monasteries, neighbourhood watch committees and 'work teams' that the Chinese authorities have set up. Beijing has also established a network of security personnel, including People's Liberation Army (PLA), People's Armed Police (PAP), Public Security Bureau (PSB) and a complex and vast network of paid informers. This anti-splittism bureaucracy employs at least about 400,000 cadres. The party through its bureaucracy has also issued various documents, directives and guidelines to control creative expression with systematic procedures to destroy and to sinocize Tibetan culture.

The communist party's inherent intolerance and repressive nature is shown in its appointment of party secretaries since its occupation of Tibet. Beginning with Zhang Jingwu (1951-1965) as the first secretary of the Chinese Communist Party in Tibet to Wu Yingjie, the current party secretary, all were Chinese, except Wu Jingua. Wu is of Yi nationality and was reportedly fired from his position in 1988 for 'right deviationism'. According to the Kashag's statement on Tibetan Democracy Day on 2 September 2000, during a closed-door meeting on Tibet in December 1999 in Chengdu, Sichuan Province, Chen Kuiyuan recommended to the Chinese government to "...eradicate Tibetan Buddhism and culture from the face of the earth so that no memory of them will be left in the minds of coming generations of Tibetans, except as museum pieces."[14] He stated that the main cause of instability is the existence of the Dalai

53

Lama and his government in exile and these must be "uprooted." He recommended that Tibet, Tibetan people and Tibetan Buddhism must be destroyed and the Tibet Autonomous Region be merged with Chinese provinces like Sichuan.

In his article *China's Gaping Wound* published in *The New Statesman* on 14 June 2007, Jonathan Mirsky writes that Hu Jintao, the former Chinese President, told him that he disliked Tibet, its lack of culture and its 'dangerous people'. Hu imposed martial law in Tibet in 1989 after a spell of peaceful protests by Tibetans in Lhasa. It was during his reign that the 10th Panchen Lama suddenly and mysteriously died in Shigatse in 1989.

Zhang Qingli, the former party boss in Tibet, described the Dalai Lama as "a wolf in monk's clothes, a devil with a human face." On 16 August 2006, during an interview with *Der Speigel*, he wondered, "I have never understood why a person like the Dalai Lama was honoured with this prize. What has he done for peace? How much guilt does he bear toward the Tibetan people! How damaging is he for Tibet and China! I cannot understand why so many countries are interested in him."[15]

He said, "The Communist Party is like the parent to the Tibetan people, and it is always considerate about what the children need. The Central Party Committee is the real Buddha for Tibetans."

More recently in 2010, he said, "If there were no anti-China forces or no Dalai to destroy and create chaos, Tibet would be better off than it is today,"[16]

Such intolerance of successive Chinese leaders to Tibetan culture deviates sharply from official policies spelled out on paper.

In principle, Beijing has sound policies on the preservation and promotion of Tibetan culture and religion as stated in the '17-Point Agreement' which says that Tibetans "shall have the freedom to develop their spoken and written language and to preserve or reform their customs, habits and religious beliefs..."[17] And the constitution of the PRC states that "all ethnic groups have the freedom to use and develop their own spoken and written languages and to preserve or reform their own folkways and customs."[18]

However, in practice due to intolerance and the Chinese leaders' perception of the existence of Tibetan culture and identity as a threat, the Chinese authorities have put together a systematic plan and execution of various campaigns and policies to annihilate Tibetan culture. These measures of social control, suppression and eventual eradication of Tibetan tradition and culture are recorded in official documents, directives and guidelines. Some of these documents are cited below.

In 1982, Beijing issued *The Basic Viewpoint and Policy on the Religious Question during Our Country's Socialist Period* (popularly known as *Document 19*). This was the most authoritative and comprehensive statement issued by China on the permissible scope of religious freedom. The document "declared religious tolerance to be a necessary step in the path towards eradication of religion."[19]

Work Plans of the Regional Party and the Regional People's Government for Resolutely Striking Splittists and Other Serious Criminals Through Screening and Investigation (referred to as *Document No. 13*) issued in July 1989, included sections on "reorganizing and strengthening the management of the monasteries" and increasing propaganda in monasteries.[20]

A Golden Bridge Leading to a New Era published by "TAR" Party in 1994 ordered a halt to any further expansion of Buddhist institutions in Tibet, and identified opposing the Dalai clique as the lifeline of TAR's struggle and advocated that 'to kill a serpent, its head must be crushed.'[21]

Document No. 5 of the Sixth Enlarged Plenary Session of the Standing Committee of the Fourth Congress of TAR Branch of the Chinese Communist Party issued on 5 September 1994, include a section on "cutting off the serpent's head," encouraging Chinese migration [into Tibet], closing monasteries, intensifying political education, and punishing people who sing so-called counterrevolutionary songs.[22]

Order No. 5 issued by the State Religious Affairs Bureau in July 2007 requires recognition of all reincarnate lamas be authorized by Beijing.[23]

Order No. 2 from the People's Government of Kardze (Ch. Ganzi) in Kham in eastern Tibet in June 2008, which, amongst many things, stated that monks and nuns "who show stubborn attitude will be counseled, strictly given warning, stripped of their rights as religious practitioners and expelled from their monasteries, and held in custody doing re-education," and that tulkus "will be stripped of their right to hold the incarnation lineage."[24]

The drastic impacts of these views and policies are explained and explored below.

Eradication of Tibetan Buddhism

"Religion is the opium of the people,"[1] wrote Karl Marx. "Religion is a spiritual oppression ... [a kind] of spiritual booze,"[2] Lenin wrote. As mentioned above in 1954 when Mao met the Dalai Lama for the last time, he whispered, "Religion is poison."[3] For this communist trinity, based on whose theories and principles the People's Republic of China operates, religion is a social toxin.

The Chinese Communist Party once stated that "since religion is harmful to the socialist construction of the mother country, it will inevitably prove harmful to the progress and development of the minority nationalities ... All national characteristics unfavourable to the socialist construction and national progress can and should be changed."[4]

These clearly indicate that the Chinese leaders view Buddhism as the biggest hurdle to their control over Tibet. In the 1950s and 60s under 'democratic reform', land and other assets were seized from the monasteries. In *A Short History of Tibet*, Hugh Richardson writes, "Attacks on religion became more violent. Lamas were assaulted and humiliated; some were put to death. The ordinary people who refused

Chinese orders to give up the practice of religion were beaten and had their goods confiscated." By 1959 the occupying Chinese forces killed a large number of monks and civilians and numerous religious structures were demolished, prompting International Commission of Jurists to comment that "they [Chinese] have systematically set out to eradicate this religious belief in Tibet," and that "in pursuit of this design they [Chinese] have killed religious figures because their religious belief and practice was an encouragement and example to others."[5]

Rick Fields in his book, *How the Swans Came to the Lake: A Narrative History of Buddhism in America*, says, "The Chinese had swiftly and brutally suppressed the revolt of 1959, a half million people lost their lives, and Tibetan culture had been nearly eradicated. Monasteries had been transformed into barracks, and many of the ancient texts of Tibetan and Indian Buddhism burned, or used as fodder for mules. To the Chinese, Buddhism and feudalism were one and the same, and both had to be destroyed."[6]

Jung Chang and Jon Halliday add, "Mao was bent on destroying religion, the essence of most Tibetans' lives. When he met the Dalai Lama in 1954-5 he told him there were too many monks in Tibet, which he said, was bad for reproducing labour force. Now lamas and nuns were forced to break their vows of celibacy and get married."[7]

Arjia Rinpoche says that in 1958 the occupying Chinese army "forced [the monks of his monastery] to assemble at Yar Nang Choedra" and "in a public accusation meeting, more than 500 monks were beaten and arrested. More cycles of arrests took place and by the end of 1958, the Three Red Flags symbolizing the Great Leap Forward, Socialism, and People's Communes were flying above Kumbum. Women were urged to come live inside the monastery's walls and marry the monks who lived there."[8]

In his historic 70,000 character petition, submitted to the Chinese Premier Zhou Enlai in 1962, the 10th Panchen Lama, writes that "the democratic campaign, which was carried out in conjunction with suppression of the rebellion, was a large-scale, fierce, acute and life-and-death class struggle, which overturned heaven and earth,"[9] during which the cadres "carried out in a muddled fashion all types of half-baked directives"[10] to arrest, accuse, lockup and heavily subject people to unfair interrogations and political education. The first task of the 'reform' was to attack religion by destroying the statues of the Buddha and burning the scriptures in the name of 'eliminating superstition'. Work teams forced monks to return to their homes and to marry. In monasteries 'democratic management committees' were set up, whose members engaged in immoral and totally anti-religious acts such as going with prostitutes, drinking excessively, and kept their hair long and as a result "religious activities were as scarce as stars in the daytime."[11]

The petition adds that Tibet in the past had "total of about 110, 000 monks and nuns ... After the democratic reform was concluded, the number of monks and nuns living in the monasteries was about 7,000 people, which is a reduction of 93% ... Due to this, the sweet dew of 'teaching, debating and writing' and 'listening, thinking and contemplating' has dried out."[12]

In the spring of 1956, Athar Norbu tells in *Buddha's Warriors: the Story of the CIA-backed Tibetan Freedom Fighters, the Chinese Invasion and the Ultimate Fall of Tibet* by Mikel Dunham, after the PLA stormed Lithang Monastery, "three Russian Ilyushin-28 warplanes circled ... and bombed Lithang. By the time they had dropped all their bombs, nothing was left ... totally gone in a matter of minutes ... all the ancient texts, the famous art, the holy relics, the stupas, the largest statue of the Buddha in Tibet ... everything was gone."[13] Over three thousand monks, nuns and lay people were killed in the siege. "Those same bombers flew to other monasteries that day, in Ba and Markham area, and destroyed them just as they had destroyed Lithang."[14]

In his essay *The End of Tibetan Buddhism*, published in *The Struggle for Tibet*, the Chinese author Wang Lixiong, who lives in Beijing, writes that a tulku educational group was established in Lhasa in 1964, "where more than ten tulkus under the age of twenty were gathered for thought reform and labour — specifically as butchers and hunters of wild animals. Some of the things learned from the study group became lifelong addiction the tulkus later had trouble shedding."[15]

Wang further writes that after 1959, the Chinese communist authorities disrupted religious activities that led to "an entire generation within the monastic community [to] become polluted in their views on religion, [and] a new generation had grown up completely in an atheist environment."[16]

On 25 August 1966 the Cultural Revolution was launched in Tibet. Two days later, Red Guards from TAR's teachers' training college put up posters and handed out leaflets ordering the eradication of feudal culture, which listed that all books praising idealism and feudalism should be prohibited; all *mani* walls, prayer flags and incense burners should be destroyed; no one should recite prayers, circumambulate, prostrate; and that all monasteries and temples apart from those that are protected by the government should be converted for general public use; and monks and nuns should be allowed to marry and that they must engage in productive labour.[17] This systematic campaign of destruction was carried across Tibet. The Cultural Revolution reached even a tiny remote village like Rivoche, where the monastery and the 13-story *stupa* built in the village by Thangtong Gyalpo, the 14th century Tibetan social reformer, were destroyed. Statues were broken down and scriptures burnt. Monks of the monastery were forced to throw the physical remains of Thangtong Gyalpo into the nearby Yarlung Tsangpo River.

In his book *Search For Jowo Mikyoe Dorjee,* Ribhur Tulku, who lived through the Cultural Revolution and underwent struggle sessions and later recovered the statue of Jowo Rinpoche from China in 1982, stated that all the scriptures in Jokhang, Tibet's holiest shrine, in Lhasa, and other monasteries were burned, and sacred objects were taken away to China either for melting or to be sold to art dealers in black markets outside of China.[18] During the Cultural Revolution, Jokhang was turned into a pigsty.

59

The late Dr Lobsang Wangyal writes that during the height of the Cultural Revolution, prisoners were struggled against and routinely beaten for engaging in anything resembling Tibetan habit or custom. "Prisoners were subjected to struggle sessions for even using spoons and wooden bowls. Using a traditional Tibetan belt earned public humiliation and beating," he says.[19]

Tsering Shakya, a contemporary Tibetan scholar and historian, writes in *Dragon in the Land of Snow: the History of Modern Tibet Since 1947* that the Cultural Revolution aimed to create a 'socialist man'. "Those who held on to old values and traditions were said to possess a 'green brain', while the progressive man had a normal 'white brain.' The new brain would be filled with the teachings of Chairman Mao. As food provided nourishment to the body, so that teachings of Mao would bring ideological transformation. It was said that without studying the *Thoughts of the Chairman Mao*, the brain would be empty."[20]

Tibet had more than 6,259 religious institutions with about 592,558 resident monks and nuns in the monasteries and nunneries, which housed hundreds and thousands of statues and religious artefacts. When Mao's Cultural Revolution ended with his death in September 1976, Chinese government was responsible for the destruction of more than 6000 monasteries.[21] The contents of these monasteries were destroyed, looted and millions of ancient and priceless manuscripts burnt.

Ribhur Tulku writes that "during the Cultural Revolution, most of the Tibetan cultural artefacts were carted to China and destroyed. The statues and ritual objects of pure gold and silver were never seen again. Those of gilded copper, bell-metal, red copper, brass, etc., were ferried to Luyen, from where they were eventually sold to foundries in Shanghai, Sichuan, Tai Yuan, Beijing etc. The foundry called Precious Metal Foundry, situated about five kilometres to the east of Beijing city, alone purchased about 600 tonnes of Tibetan crafted metals."[22] Of the 600 tonnes only 50 tonnes were later salvaged. The rest were melted and sold. This was one of the many foundries in China that purchased, melted and sold Tibetan religious artefacts.

High lamas and monks were jailed, forced into labour camps and were killed for their belief. Keutsang Tulku Jampel Yeshi, whose former incarnation led the search party that was responsible for identifying the present Dalai Lama, writes in *Memoirs of Keutsang Tulku* that once in jail he was forced to transport human excrements from toilets to the fields under 'reform through hard labour' campaign. Keutsang Tulku was beaten, forced to undergo intense political education and during the later years in prison he and inmates were made to repair bicycles and knit sweaters which were either exported or sold in markets by the authorities. His monastery was destroyed and students were either jailed or defrocked.[23]

Palden Gyatso, a monk, who spent more than three decades in jail, was also tortured, forced to undergo ideological education and put under 'reform through hard labour' campaign in the gulag in Tibet . He writes in his autobiography *Fire Under Snow: True Story of a Tibetan Monk* that he was handcuffed, legs shackled and was interrogated for days to force him to denounce his spiritual teacher, Gyen Rinzin Tenpa, who was a member of 1946 Tibetan delegation sent to India to congratulate British India on their victory in the Second World War. The Chinese authorities forced Palden Gyatso to confess that his teacher was a spy sent by the Indian Government.[24]

The measures to control and to annihilate religion stem from the fact that religion is considered the biggest threat to party rule. The various policies on religion are overseen and authorized by China's highest bodies, the Central Committee, Politburo and the State Council. The party sits at the top of a tightly controlled system that implements policies and directives in Tibet.

Through this chain of unbroken command, the Democratic Management Committee (DMC)[25] that China set up in each of the monasteries throughout Tibet implements the policies. Jin Wei, the author of *100 Questions about Tibet,* says that DMC "receives guidance and support from relevant government departments in charge of religious affairs, and keeps them informed of any problem in implementing state policies..." Through this system, the government imposes maximum economic and political control over monasteries. One of DMC's important functions is to inform the PSB of the 'identities of counter-revolutionaries'. The local DMC operates with 'work teams', a specially formed unit of government personnel sent to conduct 'patriotic re-education' in an institution or locality, to conduct political education and investigation. The 'work teams' routinely move into monasteries and nunneries sometimes for months "to carry out investigations, hold meetings, conduct surveillance and identify candidates for arrest."[26] Thus the traditional role of the lama or the abbot, who is the spiritual teacher and the final authority on all monastic issues, is undermined and the entire religious establishment is turned into a political battlefield to bend monks' and nuns' loyalty towards the party.

In 1994, *A Golden Bridge Leading to a New Era* was issued. This is the guidelines on religious policy announced at the Third Work Forum on Tibet, which gave strict orders to curtail religious activities.

A Golden Bridge states that "there are too many places where monasteries have been opened without permission from the authorities, and having too much religious activity ... the waste of materials, manpower and money has been tremendous ... sometimes leading to interference in administration, low education, marriage, birth control and daily life,"[27] and that "each monk and nun [must] give declarations of their absolute support for the leadership of the Communist Party and the integrity of the motherland."[28]

This was aimed at reshaping the thinking of the monks and nuns through political education requiring them to "draw a clear line of demarcation with the Dalai clique."[29]

The Fourth Work Forum held in 2001 concentrated on strengthening "Party building" as one of the focuses to gain support and legitimacy. Jiang Zemin said at the forum that it is important to "strengthen the administration of religious affairs, strike those who use religion to carry out splittist criminal activities, and vigorously lead Tibetan Buddhism to adapt to socialism"[30]

Beijing launched campaigns such as 'Strike Hard' and 'Patriotic Re-education' through which the government heavily interferes in the religious institutions and to introduce "Marxist outlook to Buddhism or reshaping of Buddhism to suit the needs of socialist China."[31]

A Golden Bridge states that "religious tenets and practices which do not comply with socialist society should be changed,"[32] strengthening Beijing's assertion that there cannot be two suns in the sky. There can be only one sun and that is the Communist Party. This has always been the central focus of China's policy on Tibetan Buddhism, forcing the monks and nuns 'to love the Communist Party of China; to love the motherland; to love socialism; and to love the people.'[33]

On 15 February 1996, a statement by Tibet's Commission of Nationalities and Religious Affairs issued in *Tibet Daily* stated that "we must close the doors of the lamaseries which have serious problems or where political problems often occur for overhauling and consolidation and set a time limit for correction."[34]

On 18 April 2001, after sending 'work team' officials to conduct the 'patriotic re-education' campaigns, Larung Gar Buddhist Institute in Kham in eastern Tibet was issued a notice putting a ceiling on the number of resident monks and nuns. This sprawling spiritual establishment, which was started as a hermitage in the early 1980s in order to bypass China's restrictions on the construction of new monasteries, was founded by the respected Khenpo Jigme Phuntsok. At its height Larung Gar Institute had more than 10,000 students, including more than 1000 Chinese followers. The 'work team' officials evicted over 7,000 students. In June of the same year, thousands of security officials camped on the outskirts of the Institute and destroyed the monastic residences of the evicted students. The institute's founder, Khenpo Jigme Phuntsok, was arrested. He died on 7 January 2004.[35]

Since its first demolition in 2001, Larung Gar Buddhist Institute attracted thousands of more students throughout Tibet, China, Hongkong, Taiwan and Malaysia in the subsequent years and grew to its former size in terms of students' population. Now, it is once again being subjected to the same demolition. Thousands of monks and nuns are being expelled from the academy and their homes destroyed. This ongoing demolition of the academy in eastern Tibet has been widely covered by the international media and is a cause of serious concern to Tibetans in Tibet and outside.

In December 2002, Tenzin Delek Rinpoche,[36] the founder of Kham Nalanda Monastery in eastern Tibet, was sentenced to death with a two-year reprieve on false charges of having been involved in a bombing case. The Chinese authorities de-recognised him as an incarnate lama and ordered him to become a common monk, and denied confirmation of the two reincarnations that Tenzin Delek Rinpoche had earlier recognized. Because of his work to benefit the people, Tenzin Delek Rinpoche commanded widespread respect and trust among both Tibetans and Chinese in his area. The local authorities saw this as a threat to their legitimacy and power, and had been looking for a way to remove him. That year Tulku Tenzin Delek Rinpoche was arrested and put in prison. In July 2015 he died under Chinese policy custody. The Chinese police refused to return his body to his grieving relatives for proper cremation, fearing that a respectful cremation of the body of this dynamic Tibetan spiritual leader would attract thousands of his devoted followers and this might cause social unrest in the locality.

According to the *Annual Report 2009* by United States Commission on International Religious Freedom, Tulku Phurbu Tsering, a highly respected *tulku* of Tehor Kardze Monastery in eastern Tibet , "was detained on 19 May 2008 after police detained more than fifty of his students for staging a peaceful protest against requirements that they denounce the Dalai Lama and their teacher."[37]

In 1999 Bangri Rinpoche and Nyima Choedron, who founded an orphanage in Lhasa called Gyatso Children's Home, were arrested on charges of espionage and activities endangering national security, and were sentenced to 15 and 10 years in jail respectively.[38]

Many other contemporary Tibetan religious leaders such as Geshe Sonam Phuntsok[39] of Dargay Monastery in Kardze in eastern Tibet were arrested and jailed on trumped-up charges.

These lamas and *tulkus* have moral authority and a role as unofficial community leaders who champion the welfare of Tibetans. People turn to them for guidance and advice on both religious and secular matters. This is seen as undermining the party's authority.

In mid May 2007 the Chinese authorities demolished a colossal statue of Guru Rinpoche near Samye Monastery in central Tibet and rubbles from the destroyed statue were transported to unknown locations.

According to a report by the Tibetan Centre for Human Rights and Democracy "a convoy of Chinese PAP came to Samye Monastery, Dranang County, Lhoka Prefecture, TAR, and forcibly demolished a nearly completed gold and copper plated statue of Guru Padmasambhava [Rinpoche]. The statue was constructed with the fund of about 800,000 Chinese Yuan generously donated by two Chinese devotees from the highly industrialized Mainland city of Guangzhou in Guangdong Province."[40]

In 2007, the State Religious Affairs Bureau issued the so-called *Order No. 5* that requires recognition of all reincarnate *tulkus* or lamas to be authorized by Beijing. This is a clear and direct interference in Tibetan people's spiritual domain. In this way Beijing choose to employ religion as a tool not only "to transform Tibetan national identity and loyalty to the Dalai Lama into Chinese national identity and loyalty to China"[41] but also as a kind of legal measure to put their people in positions that control and supervise the Tibetan people's spiritual activities.

This was clear from the way Beijing involved itself in the selection of the 11th Panchen Lama. Arjia Rinpoche, the former abbot of

Kumbum Monastery who now lives in exile in the US, says that he "was forced to play a part in the selection of the 11th Panchen Lama by the Chinese government. Since the government wished to use this event as a precursor to their future election of the 15th Dalai Lama, they made up their own rules and carefully choreographed the Golden Urn Ceremony. I was an eyewitness to the fact that the ritual was a farce and that the selection was rigged. It was totally manipulated."[42]

The Chinese author, Wang Lixiong, writes in *The End of Tibetan Buddhism* that the "local political power has become the only controlling force, one that obviously demands the surrenders of monks and nuns to its authority. It has nothing to do with respecting the dharma or observing monastic vows."[43]

As a result, anything to do with religion in Tibet today, including building, renovation, admission to monasteries, the limit of the number of monks in monasteries, religious festivals, and pilgrimages, has to be authorized by the Commission of Nationalities and Religious Affairs.

Beijing's systematic policies have led to executions, destruction of religious institutions, political indoctrination, expulsion of monks and nuns, imprisonment, banning religious ceremonies, restricting the number of monks in monasteries and enforcing loyalty to the party. The systematic destruction of and severe control on religion has led to the collapse of the Tibetan Buddhist civilization in Tibet.

This destruction is clearly revealed in the report issued by Beijing-based Gongmeng Law Research Centre, an organisation of independent Chinese lawyers. In the aftermath of the widespread unrest in Tibet in 2008, Gongmeng sent researchers to Tibet to find out the causes of these protests. Their findings were made public in May 2009. *Gongmeng Report* points out that Buddhism "is not only an important constituent part of Tibetan culture, it is also the main source of thinking for how Tibetan religious culture comports with the logic of historical development."[44] The report adds, "Having been through the Cultural Revolution, there's now a gap in the ages of the inheritors of religious culture in Tibetan areas, with a lack of middle-aged monks leaving a weakness in influence and transmission from older monks to younger monks."[45]

This breakdown in the transmission of Buddhism from the old to the new generation is the most fatal assault on Tibetan Buddhist culture. This in turn has led to the collapse of the special bond between spiritual masters or the lamas and their students. This special bond or *dam-tshig* is the sacred commitment that consists of maintaining harmonious relationship between masters and students and at the same time fosters the continuity of the true teachings and their practice. *Dam-tshig* consists of the vows of integrity, pledge, loyalty, and the word of honour between teachers and the students. Since the introduction of Buddhism to Tibet in the 7th century, the entire corpus of Buddhist philosophy and knowledge on astronomy, language, law and ethics were passed from one generation to the next through this unique system of learning. This becomes especially important in the practice of Buddhist tenets as many essential teachings, initiations and transmissions are orally passed from the root masters to their students.

The most respected spiritual master is the Dalai Lama, who Beijing describes as a 'separatist' and more scathingly by the former party boss in Tibet, Zhang Qinglin, as "a wolf in monk's clothes, a devil with a human face," is the supreme temporal and spiritual leader of all Tibetans. Tibetan people's devotion to, faith and trust in him are unblemished, attesting to the fact that the Dalai Lama provides spiritual guidance and able leadership when Tibet and Tibetans are facing the most pressing circumstances.

However, Beijing considers this special relationship between the Dalai Lama and his people based on complete trust, loyalty, devotion and faith as the key threat to their power and legitimacy in Tibet. The Communist Party has heightened its attacks on the Dalai Lama in the hope of severing this special bond. Tibetan monks, nuns and lay people, who display any loyalty to or show faith in the Dalai Lama are described as "the scum of Buddhism" and "the loyal running dogs of the Dalai clique."

"The influence of our enemies in foreign countries, especially the 'Dalai clique,' is slipping into the monasteries of our region more than ever"[46] states *A Golden Bridge Leading to a New Era*. In its counterattack to undermine such influence, Beijing initiated Tibet-wide 'patriotic re-education' campaign in almost all religious institutions. This has replaced traditional religious education. Now monks and nuns are forced to undergo political re-education under the strict supervision of DMC and 'work teams.'

DMC and 'work teams' conduct written exams for the monks and nuns after 'patriotic re-education' sessions. The questions in the tests include: What are the reasons to oppose separatists and the Dalai clique? What is the number one political responsibility of the TAR? What are the ways to show your love for the motherland?[47]

These questions must be answered according to the political and ideological education which the monks and nuns are forced to undergo. There are a few books on 'patriotic re-education' such as a book on opposing separatism; a book on [the Chinese version] Tibetan history; a book on conduct of citizens; and a book on government policies.[48] These books are mandatory study material in religious institutions.

Notices, the Marxist view of religion, are put on the walls of monasteries. These notices say, for example, "In a socialist society such as our own, the Marxist religious viewpoint is the theory and guide for how to understand and handle religion and questions of religion."[49] Monks and nuns are made to recite — I oppose the Dalai clique; I will not keep the Dalai's photo in my house; my thinking will not be influenced by the Dalai clique; I love the Communist Party; I will follow the Party no matter what, etc.[50]

DMC has taken the place of *khenpos* (abbots, whose responsibility before 1959 was like an academic dean of a university) and *lamas* who are traditional heads of monasteries. Political indoctrination has replaced religious education. The special bond between spiritual teachers and students has been severed and rules are enforced to limit the number and age of students. The new mandatory registration of monks and nuns does not allow students outside of the locality.[51]

In an official documents titled *Cheng Guan Qu Fa Lu Chang Shi Pu Ji Du Ben* states that the DMC must report to the local security branch about any 'activity harmful to the national security' and 'public stability' carried out by the monastery's lamas, *khenpos*, chant and discipline masters.[52]

On 28 June 2008, Li Zhangping, head of the so-called Kardze Tibetan Autonomous Prefecture, which has more political and religious prisoners than any other Tibetan region outside of the TAR, has issued an *Order No. 2*. The order instructed monks and nuns, "who do not agree to be registered and photographed, who leave the monastery premises as they please and refuse to correct themselves despite repeated re-education, will be completely expelled from the monastery, will have their rights as religious practitioners annulled, will be sent back to their native places, and their residential cells will be demolished,"[53] and "any *tulku*, *khenpo* and *geshe* who does not abide by the order will not be allowed to participate in religious activities" and "in the case of *tulkus*, they will be stripped of the right to hold the incarnation lineage."[54]

Voice of Tibet radio broadcast on 23 July 2010 says that Lama Dawa of Rongpo Chojey Monastery in Nakchu was arrested in April that year with the accusation of having links with the Dalai Lama. The Chinese authorities stripped Lama Dawa of his religious position and the right to hold the incarnation lineage. According to the same radio broadcast, 17 other monks from the same monastery were arrested under the 'patriotic re-education' campaign and ordered them to oppose the Dalai Lama and Lama Dawa. As a result a 70-year-old monk named Ngawang Gyatso committed suicide on 20 May 2010 and later all 17 monks were kicked out from the monastery. The authorities labelled this event as '5-20 Incident' and branded the monastery as 'criminal monastery' that must be watched constantly.[55]

At the same time, Wang Lixiong writes that in Tibet today, "all famous monasteries have to be transformed into tourist sites, while high-ranking tulkus are utilized as attractions for commercial investment ... That is how they became a valuable commodity."[56]

Similarly, Ma Jian, the Chinese author and painter who widely travelled in Tibet writes in his book *Stick Out Your Tongue* that "Tibet was a land whose spiritual heart had been ripped out. Thousands of temples lay in ruins, and the few monasteries that had survived were damaged and defaced. Most of the monks who'd returned to the monasteries seemed to have done so for economic rather than spiritual reasons. The temples gates were guarded by armed policemen, and the walls were daubed with slogans instructing the monks to 'Love the Motherland, love the Communist Party and study Marxist-Leninism.'"[57]

The 10th Panchen Lama clairvoyantly wrote in his 70,000 character petition in 1962 that "the future of religion has in reality been destroyed; therefore, in fact, religion has no future."[58]

The Communist Party's destruction of Tibetan Buddhist tradition and religious institutions has had a chain impact on education, Tibetan values, language and communal harmony. Tibet today experiences increased social breakdown, lawlessness, communal disharmony, illiteracy, uncontrolled greed and a high growth in sex trade and alcoholism,[59] which in turn contribute to the deterioration of Tibetan society.

Damage and Distortion in Education and Tibetan Language

Beijing's fundamental education policy in Tibet since its occupation has been to win over the loyalty of generations of Tibetans. To fulfil this task, the education strategy has been shaped by ideological viewpoint to stem any Tibetan character, identity and content.

In early 1960s the Chinese authorities started to 'reform' Tibetan language by making grammatical changes to make it closer to the so-called proletarian language as spoken by the people. The most pronounced example was the elimination of three of the five *del-dra* or genitive particles *gi, kyi, gyi, yi 'i*.[1] These were considered redundant. The standard written Tibetan requires all five.

In her book *Education in Tibet: Policy and Practice since 1950*, Catriona Bass writes that "during the Cultural Revolution, all concessions to culturally specific education for China's nationalities were abolished; the political nature of education during this period meant that it consisted almost entirely of launching attacks on the traditional Tibetan culture, the prime target being the Tibetan language."[2]

The Tibetan scholar, Muge Samten, who had first-hand experience of the occupation and had lived through the terrible decades of the Cultural Revolution, said that "almost all the universities and schools in Tibet were shut down, Tibetan language classes were banned, bits of Tibetan used in propaganda material were so-called 'reformed language' created in the name of destroying the 'four olds,' opposing the bourgeoisie and to be closer to 'people's language'. This 'reformed language' was devoid of standard Tibetan grammatical usage and was far removed from the colloquial language spoken by ordinary people. Anyone using the standard Tibetan language was attacked by having them branded as 'revisionists' and counter-revolutionary."[3]

The campaign to smash the 'olds' led to the complete destruction of traditional learning centres, banishment of intellectuals to labour camps and carrying out mass struggle sessions to cleanse people's memories of the past.

In her book *Life In the Red Flag People's Commune*, Dhondup Choedon, as a young Tibetan woman attended The Red Flag People's Commune School in Nyethang Dzong in Lhoka, southern Tibet. Later she escaped into exile in 1973, and in her book she writes, "there is a meeting once in every week where the children engage in criticism and self-criticism ... The children were asked to report any anti-Chinese remark or act they see ... The Chinese lecture them constantly about the prosperity and happiness brought by the

Chinese liberation and condemn the old society, where the 'crimes committed by the three big serf-owners cannot fit the sky.'[4]

Catriona Bass writes in her book that when the TAR Teachers' College was established in 1975, Tian Bao, deputy secretary of the TAR party committee announced: "Students should be selected from among the workers and peasants with practical experience, and they should return to production after a few years of study"[5] and that "the major topic of the new college was to be class struggle, and the curriculum was to focus on the 'ideological transformation' of the students."[6]

Liberal policies initiated in the early 1980s by Hu Yaobang and encouraged by the late Panchen Lama were emasculated by the decade's end when leftist hard-liners regained power in Tibet. Hu Jintao replaced Wu Jingua, who was widely perceived as a liberal. Hu was followed by Chen Kuiyuan, the firebrand party boss in Tibet and the "pendulum swung back to promote ideological education over academic education."[7] Chen ruled Tibet from 1992 to 2000. Robert Barnett, a Tibet scholar and a professor at Columbia University, remarked during a seminar on Tibet held in St Andrew's University in Scotland in August 2001 that Chen increased attacks on Tibetan scholars and intellectuals and played an important role in reshaping "the pedagogy of Tibetan history and culture in the University of Tibet."[8]

In his speech at the Fifth Regional Meeting on Education in the TAR on 26 October 1994, Chen announced that ideological goals must be the top priority in schools:"The success of our education does not lie in the number of diplomas issued to graduates from universities, colleges, polytechnic schools and middle schools. In the final analysis, in whether our graduating students are opposed to or turn their hearts to the Dalai clique and in whether they are loyal to or do not care about our great motherland and the great socialist cause. This is the most salient and the most important criteria for assessing right and wrong, and the contributions and mistakes of our educational work in Tibet. To successfully solve the problem, we must improve political and ideological work in schools, and have political and ideological work run through all the teaching, study and work at schools."[9]

In the same speech Chen stated that "...schools are not a forum on 'freedom'. Schools should be captured by socialism. We should not allow the splittist elements and religious idealism to use the classrooms to poison people's sons and daughters ... This is an issue which deserves our utmost concern. This is a test."[10]

Chen further made this clear. "Scriptures have entered some schools and become textbooks in the classrooms. Some students have joined the ranks of monks. Some people purposely interpret this phenomenon as a national feature in an attempt to legalise religious interference in educational affair ... Therefore, we have arduous tasks in political and ideological work as well as heavy responsibilities in training constructors (sic, perhaps instructors) and successors who possess deep love for the Motherland and socialist undertakings."[11]

Not only was there a shift in packing the curriculum with ideological content but Chen even suggested discarding subjects such as science and technical studies. This went counter to the claims by Beijing that literacy level had gone up and that all-round education was given to Tibetans. Chen said, "Ethnic education cannot be regarded as successful if it successfully maintains the old culture and traditions, but fails to suit the need of present social development."[12]

In 1994, a TAR government report instructed that "schools of all categories at various levels should firmly put the correct political orientation above all else and strive to train qualified personnel who have lofty ideals, moral integrity, a good education and a strong sense of discipline."[13] This was reiterated in *A Golden Bridge Leading to a New Era* which states that teachers "should have some professional skills, but most of all, they must be determined revolutionaries,"[14] which reveals a clear official preference for "red" over expert.

Along the same line selected Tibetan children are sent to China for secondary education and teachers from various Chinese provinces are sent to work in schools and colleges in Tibet. "The programme has a number of side effects which are likely to a negative impact ...[and] implications for the development of Tibetan language and culture ... Furthermore, since these [Chinese] teachers do not speak Tibetan (many of them are unable to speak even standard Chinese, *putonghua),* additional learning difficulties are created for Tibetan students."[15]

This lack of real education is confirmed by the fact that a large number of young Tibetans, risking their lives, continue to come to India to receive a decent education. Since the 1980s hundreds of thousands of Tibetans have come out of Tibet into exile, most of them are young monks, nuns and students to study in Tibetan exiles' monasteries, nunneries and schools.[16]

Gongmeng Report states that "majority of Tibetans born in the 1980s were educated to the level of elementary schools, the levels of education among the young people of our [researchers] own generation are far lower than Han areas.[17]" The report said that according to 2007 statistics, "the average term of education in Tibetan areas is less than four years, and the high-school enrolment rate is extremely low[18]" and that "majority of adults at the grass-roots are illiterate.[19]" The report states that the quality of teachers and standard of education are also low and children of nomads and farmers have difficulty in having access to education.[20]

In the beginning of 2010 the Chinese education department issued a new notice, writes Woeser, a Tibetan writer living in Beijing, which instructed "all the schools in the country to organise their students to participate in an event during Spring Festival 'wishing the beloved motherland a happy and prosperous New Year.[21]'" At the "congratulating the motherland[22]" event, the students were told to praise the legendary early ancestors, Yan and Huang Emperors; and to praise the revolutionary martyrs. The education department instructed all schools to organise the worshipping of the Yan and the Huang Emperors. Yan and Huang are considered by the Chinese to be their earliest ancestors.

At the same time, the Chinese authorities made it mandatory in schools in Tibet to have a flag-raising ceremony each morning. Peter Hessler, a veteran reporter and the author of *Country Driving: A Chinese Road Trip,* who travelled to Tibet, writes in his essay *Tibet Through Chinese Eyes* published in *The Atlantic Online* in February 1999 that he witnessed a "flag-raising ceremony at a middle school, where students and staff members lined up to listen to the national anthem, after which, in unison, they pledged allegiance to the Communist Party, [and] love for the motherland."[23]

Such systematic programming and structured methods of education leave little room for Tibetans growing up in Tibet to learn their language and find their cultural roots. As a result, generations of Tibetans grow up as hybridised species uprooted from their cultural origin and unable to adjust to the new cultural and social milieu created by the authorities.

Gongmeng Report states the "largest shortfall of teachers in Tibetan areas today is in Tibetan language.[24]" Through its research in many Tibetan areas Gongmeng found that the students find it easier to learn Chinese than Tibetan simply because of lack of qualified teachers and teaching aids. "Even though they could speak Tibetan, there were however extremely few teachers who could undertake the teaching of Tibetan, and give in-depth explanations of the Tibetan language to the students,[25]" says the report.

This lack of competent Tibetan teachers is made worse by intentional suppression of Tibetan language as testified by the detained Tibetan author Tashi Rabten or Theurang in his book *Written in Blood*. He was released after four years in April 2014. Theurang says in his book that when he was a student at Northwest University for Nationalities in Lanzhou in 2008, he and his friend put up notices about a book sale written in Tibetan on the campus walls and near the dormitories. Later they found out that all their notices were taken down while similar notices written in Chinese were left untouched. He writes, "I later found out that it was the government order to not allow any notices written in Tibetan to be put up. If any notice written in

75

Tibetan is put up, the school police were given the authority to take them down."[26]

The late professor Dungkar Lobsang Trinley, a leading Tibetan intellectual, remarked that "all hope in our future, all other developments, cultural identity, and protection of our heritage depends on this [Tibetan language]. Without educated people in all fields, able to express themselves in their own language, Tibetans are in danger of being assimilated."

Other Tibetans are equally concerned about the fate of the Tibetan language and education system in Tibet. *Tibet Under Communist China: 50 Years*, published by the Department of Information and International Relations in 2001 carries a long note of anguish by the late Khenpo Jigme Phuntsok, the founder and abbot of Larung Gar Buddhist Institute in Serta in eastern Tibet. In 1996, Khenpo Jigme Phuntsok wrote:

"Actually, the Tibetan language has no value in present-day Tibet. For instance, if a letter were mailed with an address written in Tibetan, it wouldn't reach its destination even within Tibet, let alone outside. In case of travels, no matter how literate a person is in Tibetan, he would not be able to know the bus timing or read the seat number on his ticket. Even if one has to look for a hospital or a shop in the county headquarters or a city, the knowledge of Tibetan is useless. A person who knows only Tibetan will find it difficult even to buy daily necessities.[27]

"If our language is useless in our own country, where else will it have any use? If the situation remains like this much longer, the Tibetan language will become extinct one day... Rare in Tibet are schools where one can study Tibetan language and culture ... Moreover, parents have developed the habit of not sending their children to school. This is because the primary school teaches Chinese rather than Tibetan. Even if the students learn Chinese and graduate from the middle school, there is no employment scope in Tibet. There is, of course, a slight opportunity for learning Tibetan. But the parents know that Tibetan language is useless in day-to-day life. Therefore, they have no motivation to send children to school.[28]

"In the cities and county headquarters there are serious cases of people being unable to speak Tibetan, although both their parents are Tibetans. Many of them have lost their Tibetan characteristics. Moreover, Tibetan officials cannot speak pure Tibetan. One-fifth or two-thirds of the words they use are Chinese. That's why ordinary Tibetans can't understand their speech."[29]

A report by Human Rights in China titled *China: Minority Exclusion, Marginalization and Rising Tensions* says that Tibetan children are "subjected to an educational system systematically designed to deny them the opportunity and ability to learn their own histories and languages"[30] and "to indoctrinate children and instil a sense of inferiority regarding Tibetan culture, religion and language relative to Chinese culture."[31]

Such negative impacts of the Chinese government-sponsored education are made worse by Beijing's persecution of Tibetan scholars and intellectuals through torture, arbitrary arrests and lengthy jail sentences. This trend, which decreased in the early 1980s, was reinstated and intensified during Chen Kuiyuan's rule.

In January 1996, Chen made a statement at an internal meeting saying that Tibetan nationalism was rooted in Tibetan religion, and that Tibetan religion was rooted in Tibetan culture and language. In his paper *The Chinese Frontiersman and the Winter Worms - Chen Kuiyuan in the TAR, 1992-2000* presented at St Andrews University in Scotland in 2001, Robert Barnett writes that "this theory implied that Tibetan culture and language had to be restricted,"[32] and that "shortly afterwards, the experimental Tibetan-medium school classes that had been started by the [late] Panchen Lama some six years earlier in four secondary schools were closed down."[33]

Such attitude to Tibetan language and culture was followed by crackdown on any assertion of Tibetan identity by Tibetan intellectuals and writers. In 2004, the Tibetan author and poet Woeser's book

Notes on Tibet was banned by the Chinese authorities and she was dismissed from her position as the editor Lhasa-based Chinese language journal *Tibetan Literature*.[34] The authorities instructed that all her working hours would be devoted to political re-education. Later her blog was hacked and shutdown. International PEN writes on its website that Woeser has suffered repeated and sustained harassment since 2004, including brief detentions, periods of house arrest, travel restrictions, loss of work, denial of access to information and communications, heavy surveillance and censorship.[35]

A Raging Storm: The Crackdown on Tibetan Writers and Artists after Tibet's Spring 2008 Protests, a report released by the International Campaign for Tibet, a Tibet advocacy group based in Washington, DC, in May 2010 details "the cases of more than 50 Tibetans, including 13 writers, involved in the arts and public sphere who are either in prison, have been 'disappeared' or have faced torture or harassment due to expressing their views."[36]

These intellectuals and writers include eighty-one-old Paljor Norbu, a professional printer and prominent Tibetan cultural figure in Lhasa, who was sentenced to seven years in prison for allegedly printing prohibited materials, Rinchen Sangpo, the author of *No Retreating Path* and two unpublished books *The Story of Blood* and *The Story of Lhasa*, who was beaten and tortured by the Chinese authorities in August 2006, and Kunchok Tsephel, the founder of the influential Tibetan literary website, *Chomey* or *Butter Lamp* who was sentenced to 15 years in prison by the Intermediate People's Court of Kanlho in Tso, northeastern Tibet, on charges of disclosing state secrets after a closed-door trial.[37]

Other persecuted Tibetan writers include Drogru Tsultrim, Jamyang Kyi, Dolma Kyab, Kunga Tsayang or Gangnyi and Tashi Rabten or Theurang.

Drogru was accused of sedition and supporting 'motivations of Dalai supporters' in his articles and the authorities banned the publication of his Tibetan-language journal *Khawai Tsesok* or *Lifeline of the Snow*.

Jamyang Kyi, a writer and singer, was detained by PSB in April 2008. Dolma Kyab, the author of *Restless Himalayas,* is believed to be held in Chushul high-security prison near Lhasa. Kunga Tsayang or Gangnyi, a writer, photographer and blogger, was sentenced to five years in jail in a closed-door trial on 12 November 2009 by the Kanlho Intermediate People's Court in Tso, northeastern Tibet. Tashi Rabten or Theurang, the author of *Written in Blood* and the editor of *Eastern Snow Conch Mountain* (Tib. *Shar Dungri),* a collection of essays about 2008 peaceful protests in Tibet, is believed to be in detention in Chengdu, the capital of Sichuan province in China.

A Tibetan writer to be arrested is Shogdung (Morning Conch) or Tagyal, who was arrested on 23 April 2010. He was a staff at the Nationalities Publishing House in Xining and authored many books, including his latest *The Line Between Sky and Earth,* which is about the 2008 protests in Tibet. According to the ICT's report, "his detention followed the publication of a book about the meaning of what he terms 'peaceful revolution' and the significance of the protests across Tibet since March, 2008, which he describes as: 'a sign of the rediscovery of the consciousness of nationality, culture and territory.'"[38]

The same report says that "for the first time since the end of the Cultural Revolution in 1976, singers, artists and writers have been the target of a drive against Tibetan culture in which almost any expression of Tibetan identity not validated by the state can be branded 'splittist'" and banned."[39]

There is a clear historical precedent in Manchuria, after the Qing dynasty collapsed in 1911, where "the teaching of Manchu was abolished"[40] by the Chinese authorities in the same year. "The current population of Manchu in China is nearly 10 million"[41] and yet "fewer than 100 people can speak Manchu,"[42] and scholars believe that "oral Manchu will disappear in five to 10 years."[43]

Tibet is likely to suffer the same fate with arbitrary arrests, torture, detention and long jail terms given to Tibetan writers and intellectuals getting increasingly frequent especially after 2008 uprising in Tibet. These systematic and sustained assaults stifle Tibetan language and identity, and thwart any assertion of Tibet's distinct civilization and culture based on creative expression, individual talent and collective voice.

Tibetan language is increasingly marginalized due to shrinking space for its use and China's policies are threatening to make it redundant beyond cultural and literary spheres. According to linguist, Nocolas Tournadre, associate professor of linguistics, University of Paris 8, at a roundtable before the Congressional Executive Commission on China on teaching and learning Tibetan, voiced his concerns about the future of Tibetan language, he said: "By excluding Tibetan from the administrative spheres and giving Chinese a predominant position at school and university, by offering only a handful of professional openings based on the command of Tibetan, the authorities have contributed to giving Tibetan the image of a "useless" language. The Tibetans, who have a very pragmatic approach and a great sense of adaptation, have quickly turned away from their own language."[44]

This has placed many Tibetan parents in deep dilemma, where on one hand they would want their children to be the guardian of Tibet's culture and its heritage. On the other hand, shrinking space to use Tibetan language and sheer lack of opportunities makes learning Chinese language the only way to seek employment in almost all avenues of employment.

The problem was illustrated in a widely shared blog by a celebrated Tibetan educator and social entrepreneur, Jigme Gyaltsen, during a speech he gave at the annual Political Consultative Conference held in Xining. His efforts in educating rural Tibetans earned laurels and was profiled in the state-sponsored broadcasting channel, CCTV, describing him as a "teacher nonpareil." In his speech he conveyed his thoughts on Tibetan language, education and society. In extraordinary detail, Jigme Gyaltsen outlines what he saw as problems with education in Tibet today, from the shortage of teachers to the language of instruction. [45]

During the six-day long conference, two expanded meetings in today's Qinghai province, Jigme Gyaltsen, a teacher, expressed some opinions on education. He said: "It's a mistake that in most schools in Tibetan areas, only Tibetan language class is taught in Tibetan and other subjects such as maths, natural and social sciences etc, are taught in Chinese. The goal of a student's study is to attain a knowledge of the subjects he has learnt and to be able to put this knowledge to use. Whatever race you may be, being taught in your mother tongue instead of two languages leads to a much easier personal experience."

He further argues, "for example, if all Chinese students in Xining were taught maths, natural and social sciences etc, from textbooks written in English, we can estimate they would not pass. Furthermore, students from Tibetan areas will in future generally go on to serve Tibetans living in Tibetan areas. And because of this the production and expansion of these students who have been educated in Tibetan, is the sole means of developing education, economy and philosophy in Tibetans areas in the future."

Relying on China's census data published in the year 1990, in certain regions predominantly populated by Tibetans, even in regions where 95.46% of its population being Tibetan, medium of instruction used in most of the schools in the region are in Chinese.[46] Moreover, the fate of Tibetan language was further jeopardized after the demise of the tenth Panchen Lama, who had been championing for the rights of Tibetan people and was at the forefront of a movement to persevere Tibetan language.[47] Since 1997, Tibetan language came under yet another assault from a policy to implement the introduction of Chinese language even as early as grade one, which was earlier deemed appropriate even for grade three by the authorities in the Tibet Autonomous Region. [48]

A blanket approach to marginalize Tibetan language in regions inhabited by Tibetans had compelled young students to take to the streets to protest. In a meeting of the Education Department of Qinghai province, the Communist Party Secretary and the Chairman ordered that the language used in textbooks should be changed to Chinese.

The statement was given by the then Party Secretary of Qinghai province, Qiang Wei, made available in English by the International Campaign for Tibet, speaking at a conference in education in September he was quoted saying : "Qinghai province has vigorously implemented state common language [Chinese] teaching in compulsory education while extending the 'bilingual' teaching of minority languages and scripts, making people of all minority nationalities grasp and use the Chinese language and script, thereby achieving 'intercommunication between ethnics and Han' [minhan jiantong]." He added that strengthening ,bilingual' education, which asserts the importance of the Chinese language, is "an important political duty."

This sparked a spontaneous protest on 20th October 2010, where at least 1,000 Tibetan students in Tibet protested against the erosion of their culture and language.[49] The scale and geographical spread of protests took the authorities by surprise. The same concerns were echoed in a series of protests staged in different Tibetan regions. Following these protest, reports emerge of similar protests staged in other regions of Tibet.[50]

The Guardian on 20 October, 2010 ran a piece, citing a former teacher from the region, and now based in exile, he was quoted saying: "The Chinese are enforcing reforms which remind me of the Cultural Revolution. This reform is not only a threat to our mother tongue, but is in direct violation of the Chinese constitution which is meant to protect our rights."[51]

The Tibetan protests struck right at the heart of China's administration, in Beijing, when a group of Tibetan students in Beijing raised their concerns over threats posed to Tibetan language in tandem with other protests in Tibetan regions. On 22 October in the same year, several hundred Tibetan students in Beijing's Central University for Nationalities held a peaceful demonstration, which

T*he Guardian* described the incident as "rare" as it took the concerns to China's capital.

On 27th of January, 2016, Tashi Wangchuk, a shopkeeper was picked up by the Chinese authorities from his home. He was sharing his living space with his elderly parents in Kyegudo in northeastern Tibet. In May 2015, he took it upon himself to file a formal complaint against the authorities in his region for failing to support Tibetan language education by making a trip to Beijing. During his visit, he met with *Times* journalists and insisted on doing -- according to the paper -- "on-the-record interviews."[52]

The journalists from the *Times* followed it up by visiting Tashi Wangchuk in his hometown in September 2015 and published articles detailing his efforts along with a nine-minute video in November 2015.[53] In the video he is shown travelling with the journalists and airing his views about the status of Tibetan language.

Instead of giving a fair hearing to his concerns, he was charged in March 2016 for "inciting separatism," and faces up to 15 years in prison. Although in his interviews with the *Times* he explicitly stated that he was not advocating for Tibetan independence, and that he was mainly concerned about cultural preservation. "My goal is to change things a little bit, to push to preserve some of our nation's culture," he told the *Times*.

A defense lawyer for Tashi Wangchuk later told the *New York Times* that the case against his client focused on the interviews with the paper and that "the police were especially incensed by the video."

The Destruction of the Nomadic Way of Life

In the spring of 1956, Zhu De, Commander-in-Chief of the People's Liberation Army (PLA) and the Vice-Chairman of the Communist Party, ordered that "all nomadic herdsmen [in Tibet] should settle in order to facilitate socialist transformation and socialist construction."[1] This was during the height of enforcing 'democratic reform' in eastern and north-eastern Tibet, where majority of the agricultural sector was 'collectivised.' Massive propaganda was done to promote policy of 'mutual aid and co-operation' in the pastoral areas. The principal objective was neither to improve the lives of nomads and farmers nor to bring a positive social transformation as idealised in socialist theory. It was to enforce control, to manage and to implement the 'democratic reform' across Tibetan society. This was apparent from the official document *Outline of the Propaganda for CCP Tibetan Working Committee Concerning the Policy of Not Implementing Democratic Reforms in Tibet Within Six Years*. This document states that "to be able to live happily, the Tibetan people must take the road of socialism; and to enforce democratic reform is the unavoidable path the Tibetan people have to follow."[2] To make the nomads to settle in permanent homes and to prevent them from pasturing their herds of yaks across vast distances depending on where the grass was greener were done so that the Chinese communist authorities could better control these nomads.

In *Communalization in a Single Stride*, Xie Zhanru, first secretary, CCP Committee, Gannan Tibetan Autonomous Zhou in present Gansu stated that by 15 September, 1958 "46,000 Tibetan herdsmen, who only a short time ago still basically lived in a feudalistic society, have now, on the basis of having scored victories in the suppression of counter-revolutionaries and carried out a social reform, ... singing and dancing, have reached heaven in one stride, taking them into People's Communes in which are carried the seeds of communism."[3] Xie added that "the culture of the pastoral people is quite backward, and their level of science and technology even lower,"[4] and claimed that "after a few years of socialist ideological education by the Party, they abolished their superstitions, liberated their thoughts, promoted their class consciousness, determined to follow the socialist road."[5]

However, the dark side of the revolution imposed in the pastoral areas was that it was 'a very violent class-struggle of life and death.'[6] For Tibetans the commune system was as alien a concept as the coming of the Chinese communists who destroyed the way of life of the Tibetan nomads, who pastured their herds with the change of seasons and lived in harmony with the natural environment.

These fiercely independent nomads in their new circumstance found it hard to operate as everything was imposed from top down. "In the people's commune," Tibetans said to one another, "every person only has three personal belongings, a set of clothes, a set of bedclothes, and a bowl with a pair of chopsticks."[7]

Since ancient times, Tibetan nomads and farmers engaged in barter system in which nomads gave salt, butter, meat, dried cheese and wool in exchange for barley, clothes and other items of daily use. By the end of 1950s this way of life was replaced by the commune system, which allowed the authorities to operate a more efficient system of taxation. The taxes included, as stated elsewhere in this report, the Patriotic Grain Tax, State Grain Reserve, War Preparation Reserve[8] etc., resulting in grain shortage, and the people had to slaughter and eat much of their livestock. The late Panchen Lama writes in his 70,000 character petition that "most of the households were ransacked, and almost all of the residents' own stores of grains, meat and butter were taken away ... many of the residents were short of grain; some ran out of grain, and were very short of meat, butter, oil and so on; there was not even any lamp oil. Even firewood could not be bought."[9]

Like other Tibetans, the nomads suffered through the next three decades, which saw one political campaign after another. These campaigns culminated in the Cultural Revolution. However, the biggest threat to the way of life of Tibetan nomads is their permanent resettlement that the Chinese authorities are pushing forward with such revolutionary vigour these days.

The permanent settlement of Tibetan nomads that seriously began in the 1990s is associated with the 'Western Development' campaign. Claiming environmental protection as the reason for the fencing off of pastureland and of sedentarization of nomads, the Chinese government carried out policies such as "convert farmland to forest"[10] and "revert pasture to grassland."[11] The Chinese authorities wanted to reverse the supposed degradation in pastoral regions by imposing ban on grazing. Official policy blames the supposed crisis in the grassland on the 'primitive' and 'unscientific' way of life of the Tibetan nomads.[12]

An estimated 2.25 million nomads live on the Tibetan Plateau. For ages the Tibetan nomads skilfully managed their livestock and sustained the land while adapting to the realities of Tibet's fragile ecological system.[13] The current crisis in the pastoral regions grows out of Beijing's policies in the past 50 years, such as compulsory collectivization, imposition of production quotas, and collectivised herding which led to famine, degradation of grasslands and destruction of the traditional sustainable methods of pasture management.

In June 2007, the New York-based Human Rights Watch issued a report on the permanent re-settlement of the nomads in Tibet titled *No One Has the Liberty to Refuse*. This report explains China's nomadic resettlement project. It says, "Since 2002, the Chinese government has been implementing resettlement, land confiscation, and fencing policies in pastoral areas inhabited primarily by Tibetans, drastically curtailing their livelihood. The policies have been especially radical ... many Tibetan herders have been required to slaughter most of their livestock and move into newly-built housing colonies in or near towns, abandoning their traditional way of life.[14]

"These requirements are part of a broader policy associated with the 'Western Development' campaign. Since this campaign got underway in 1999 many Tibetan agricultural communities have had their land confiscated, with minimal compensation, or have been evicted to make way for mining, infrastructure projects, or urban development."[15]

The Human Rights Watch report quotes a Tibetan who assesses the impact of this scheme on the nomadic way of life. He says, "They are destroying our Tibetan (herding) communities by not letting us live in our area and thus wiping out our livelihood completely, making it difficult for us to survive in this world, as we have been (herders) for generations. The Chinese are not letting us carry on our occupation and forcing us to live in Chinese-built towns, which will leave us with no livestock and won't be able to do any other work."[16]

In 2003 a total ban was imposed on grazing in Golok in north-eastern Tibet and nomads were forced to move into government-built houses. A case in point that illustrates the compulsory change in land use is Tang Karma project in Amdo (Ch. Qinghai) province, where nomads are forced to resettle at a disused prison site, where there is no drinking water and electricity.[17]

The site of this project is a mixed farming settlement where nomads, who have no experience in cultivating fields and growing crops, are to engage in farming with no drinking water. A Tibetan interviewed by Human Rights Watch said in *No One Has the Liberty to Refuse* that the order came directly from the central government and not something made up [at lower levels] and that "not a single household can stay behind."[18]

Removal and relocations are also taking place to make way for large-scale infrastructural projects such as dams, mining and other undertakings like Lhasa-Xining highway. According to the research paper *Constructing A Green Railway on the Tibet Plateau: Evaluating the Effectiveness of Mitigation Measures* by Zhou Jinxing, Chinese Academy of Forestry Sciences, Yang Jun, Department of Landscape Architecture and Horticulture, Temple University in Philadelphia and Peng Gong, Beijing Normal University, the construction of the Lhasa-Xining highway was done "without an environmental impact assessment or any environment protection plan"[19] which resulted in "the destruction of the vegetative mat on the route of the highway, the adjacent vegetative mats were damaged as the soil was scraped up to build the road."[20] They add that "the damaged vegetation has led to the loss of organic matter in the soil and the melting of the permafrost layer under the topsoil."[21]

These development plans and infrastructural projects are urban-centric and finance is channelled in such a way that "Tibetans find it hard to compete with Chinese migrants."[22] In *Perversities of*

Extreme Dependence and Unequal Growth in the TAR, Andrew Fischer, a development economist who specialises on Tibet, writes that "this situation arises precisely because of who controls the subsidies and investments and where the money is spent."[23]

Fencing off of pastures, limit imposed on herds and relocation in permanent settlements have forced the nomads to seek other sources of income for which they either do not have enough skills or lack opportunities.[24] The relocation of the nomads in permanent settlements has severed their intimate connection with their animals, and rendered their knowledge of animal and grassland management, inherited from one generation to another, useless.

The officially stated reason for the permanent settlement of the nomads, from the time Zhu De ordered that "all nomadic herdsmen should settle"[25] in 1956 to the total ban on grazing in Golok and resettlement of nomads in Tibet today, is to transform the 'backward' nomads and to bring them 'scientific development'.

This assertion of bringing 'scientific development' to the nomads is particularly odd given the fact that Tibet had a long history of environment protection and respect for the land, animals and natural resources.[26]

According to Katherine Morton, a China specialist at the Australia National University, over 700,000 nomads have been resettled since 2000.[27] The official Chinese media mention that 226, 302 houses were built for Tibetan herders and farmers since early 2006[28] and that by the end of 2009 over 80 percent of herdsmen and farmers will live in houses, and the projected figure for 2009 is about 1.32 million people, or 220,000 households.[29]

The nomads were often either made a one-time payment for their livestock and are given houses with no job prospect and steady source of income.[30] As a result they resort to collecting and selling *yartsa gunbu* (summer grass and winter worm) or caterpillar fungus, a medicinal root that has high demand and very high market value. During the summer almost the entire population in nomadic area scour the grasslands for this plant.[31] In some areas local leaders issue passbooks that allow people to collect the root and then officials act as middlemen in selling it to make huge profits. Some officials organize video nights in the mountains for root collectors during which adult films are shown and cheap alcohol is sold. There were also cases of violent and often fatal conflicts over trading and scarcity as Jonathan Watts reports in the 17 June 2010 issue of *The Guardian* that "in July 2007 eight people were shot to death and 50 wounded in one such conflict."[32]

Another assault on nomads' traditional values and religious sentiments is the building of series of slaughter houses[33] in pastoral areas by the Chinese government and setting quotas for each household to provide animals to these houses. Punishments are meted out by local officials if herders fail to comply with the order to slaughter animals. In Sershul county in Kardze in eastern Tibet, people petitioned the local authorities against the slaughter house built in the locality. When the petition was rejected some monks of Bumnyak Monastery and people wrote an appeal saying that "there is no greater harm to Buddhist religion than this. Even if we don't protect living creatures, slaughtering them without mercy is against Buddhism. This is the heartfelt wish of the people."[34] The official response was to arrest the three people, who went to submit the appeal.

Summary solutions like arrests, imprisonment and coercions are compounded by large-scale resource extractions and rampant commercialisation of livestock such as yak sperm bank[35] to breed bigger yaks at a shorter time. Yaks are restricted in barbed-wire fences and herders in state-built houses.[36] The fundamental problem is the failure to acknowledge and understand the wisdom and sophistication of Tibetans' traditional livestock management, which has allowed nomads to thrive for centuries.

Wu Ning, a rangeland expert at the Chengdu Institute of Biology writes that "simply focusing on pasture or livestock development fundamentally ignores the tight linkages between culture and the land."[37] In this current policy from Beijing, nomads are at the receiving end. Chinese government has little or no experience in pastoral production and management beyond a simplistic and risky policy of reliance on overstocking, and in more recent years, on accelerated slaughter.

Traditionally in Tibet the nomads were regarded as the naturally well off. They, like most Tibetans, fervently engaged in religious activities by inviting monks and lamas, and were generous in their offerings to the monasteries. However, as the resettlement has driven them into poverty and desperation, social linkages are broken down and traditional values abandoned for immediate and the urgent need to survive.

Beijing accuses that "their [Tibetan nomads] way of life is threatening the environment" and that they live a 'primitive' life' bound by traditional concept' of self-sufficiency and "did not know how to make money by selling their domestic animals."[38] What is actually being threatened and driven into extinction is the nomads' way of life, their culture, religion and who they are as people who have successfully survived on the Tibetan Plateau for thousands of years.[39]

According to China's 2010 census report, the population of "Tibetans in China" is about 6.2 million. Out of which 2.7 million now live in the so-called Tibet Autonomous Region, and the rest, 3.5 million live in today's dismembered Tibet in provinces of Sichuan, Gansu, Qinghai and Yunnan.[39]

The Chinese government started implementing various policies to build "New Socialist Countryside" in Tibetan areas aimed at increased control of Tibetan farmers and sedentarizing Tibetan herders. In the Tibet Autonomous Region, under the policy of "Comfortable Housing," a large scale rehousing of Tibetans is carried out. And in another policy which is predominantly carried out in Amdo and in the historical eastern parts of Tibet to sedentarize nomadic herders. The Chinese government claims that these policies to all intents and purposes are to improve the quality of life and improve domestic economy.[40]

Likewise, under "Environmental Migration Schemes," in northeastern Tibet alone, the Chinese government had relocated and resettled over 300,000 Tibetans since early 2000s. Plans are afoot to resettle over 90% of nomads in the region.[41]

On November 2012, Xinhua, the official news agency of the Chinese government carried a report, citing official sources that over 737,000 nomads have been resettled out of the "headwaters region of the Yellow River over the past five years as part of efforts to protect China's "mother river" from over-grazing." [42]

A similar report on the Chinese state-run media, CCTV on 13 September, 2012 reported that: "according to the statistics, over one million Tibetan herders have bid farewell to their centuries-old nomadic lifestyle and settled down in towns and cities during the past few years…. Tibet plans to invest 400 million Yuan more in nomads' settlement of 13.4 thousands households in the approaching five years during the "Twelfth Five-Year" plan period of China."[43]

The UN Special Rapporteur on the Right to Food, Olivier De Schutter, in his report *Mission to China,* highlighted the issues surrounding the nomadic resettlement in Tibet. On the estimate of Tibetans affected by this policy he writes: "Assessing the precise number of resettled herders and rural residents is difficult, both because local authorities are encouraged to overestimate their achievements compared to official targets, and because a number of resettled herders move back to their pastures after recognising the impossibility of sustaining a decent livelihood in resettlement camps, while others migrate to cities in the hope of finding better livelihood opportunities.

"However, it was reported in 2010 that between 50 and 80 percent of the 2.25 million nomads on the Tibetan plateau were being progressively relocated."[44]

In a comprehensive report published by the Human Rights Watch in June 2013, titled *They Say We Should be Grateful : Mass Rehousing and Relocation in Tibetan Areas of China,* it details the staggering scale and speed of mass relocation in Tibet. In the course of China's modern history, the report describes, Tibetan rural population being remodelled by these policies is "unprecedented in the post-Mao era."[45]

The 'Western Development' Strategy

Since its first announcement in 1999,[46] the 'Great Opening of the West' development strategy had evolved and according to documents issued in the year 2001, it includes over 71% of China's total area that make up only 29% of its population. In the document issued in 1999, it is intended to benefit ten provincial-level regions.[47]

The Great Opening of the West is planned to be implemented over the course of 50 years in three phases. The initial phase was scheduled from 2001 to 2010, where the focus was largely on building infrastructure, health care, schooling system and strengthening the accessibility of state broadcast in rural areas. [48]

The second phase of this campaign, which is scheduled to be implemented from the year 2010 to 2030. During this second phase, the focus would be trained on accelerating economic and 'cultural development.' And in the final phase of the campaign, it would be to lift up the living standards of the population in the west on par with the rest of China.

The New Socialist Countryside and the Comfortable Housing Campaign

A new radical approach to renovate and remodel rural Tibetan housing in the TAR as part of nation-wide initiative to "Build a New Socialist Countryside" was taking shape in 2005, which according to an official document says, it is an effort to improve "the production and living condition of farmers and herdsmen, and increase their income."[49]

The "Comfortable Housing" policy was formally launched in 2006 to carry out renovation or reconstruction of private residences. It was made official as this policy appeared in the government's 11th Five-Year plan (2006-2010), which aims to ensure that 80% of Tibetan farmers and herders in the TAR would live in "safe and suitable" housing within five years. [50]

This policy is staggering in terms of number of Tibetans directly affected since its implementation. According to figures cited in official media, under this policy, TAR's government met the target to move over "2.1 million Tibetans ...to new houses or rebuilt houses from 2006 to 2012." This also went with an announcement by the TAR's government to rehouse and relocate 185,000 rural households, which amounts to about 900,000 people within three years.[51]

The Leapfrog Development Strategy

Top leadership associated with governing Tibet met during the Fifth National Work Forum on Tibet, convened by the central government in July 2010. [52] It was supposedly to introspect and frame policies after mass peaceful Tibetan protests throughout Tibet in 2008. They maintained that there was no major flaws in ongoing policies in Tibet and had "been proved entirely correct." However, the government felt the need to implement a more vibrant and ambitious rapid-growth strategy, which was termed "Leapfrog Development Strategy."

The then Party Secretary of the TAR, Zhang Qingli, in an interview outlined this new strategy, which could be pushed through with even larger investment to spur economic growth and further plans to reorganize the Tibetan countryside. This strategy aimed at bringing the per-capita net income of herders and nomads "close to the national level" by 2020.[53]

This strategy resonated right to the top Chinese leadership as the then President of the PRC, Hu Jintao, was quoted in the state media saying that the "Leapfrog Development Strategy" includes "combination of economic growth, well-off life, a healthy eco-environment, and social stability and progress."[54]

One of the key aspects of the "Leapfrog Development Strategy" is the establishment of "New Socialist Villages," renovation and relocation of Tibetan herders and nomads. This strategy seemed to stem from growing frustration within the authorities in Tibet over perceived slow progress and in order to accelerate developmental projects in Tibet.

In addition to China's plan to relocate 900,000 Tibetans by the end of 2016, [55]in a move to completely rid its region of herders and nomads, the Qinghai government announced in 2009 to settle all herders in its province, which is over a half a million Tibetans, by 2014. [56]

Challenges faced by Tibetans who are affected by these policies are documented in two comprehensive reports on the same issue by the Human Rights Watch. In its report published in 2013, *They Say We Should be Grateful*, it documents testimonies drawn from their on-field interviews in Tibet. Other than inevitable large scale embezzlement of public funds by the authorities, Tibetans speak of coerced expulsion from their grassland and homes, inadequate consultation and compensation and real threat to their culture and way of life. [57]

One such expression of grief that resonated with its readers in Tibet and even the cadres, is an essay that appeared in a popular website within Tibet, *Na Shon Sar Pa (New Tibetan Youth)*. The author of the essay who has adopted the pen name Bongtak Rilu, writes eloquently about the challenges facing Tibetan nomads affected by nomadic resettlement policies. His essay, written in earthy nomadic style, outlines *Eight Losses Faced by Tibetan Nomads* due to China's resettlement policy. Although no longer existing in its original website, a translation is available on the website of the Tibetan Centre for Human Rights and Democracy, the premier Tibetan rights group in exile.[58] Here we reproduce the english translations of the five of the *Eight Losses Faced by Tibetan Nomads* as expressed by Bongtak Rilu:

94

Loss of independent livelihood

Since ancient times, drogpas (nomads) have depended on livestock for their living. They have been used to eating dried meat, butter, cheese, milk, yoghurt and tsampa. These have become their staple diets. Moreover they survive on animal produces such as sheep wool, yak skin, cow dung and so on. They make tents, quilts and mattresses out of yak hide. Milk and yoghurt gave them a robust health. Yak and sheep dung fuel their hearths. With resettlement in urban areas, drogpas have been deprived of their traditional sources of living and staple diets. Now drogpas have to visit Chinese streets (gya sang) to buy milk, yoghurt, cheese and firewood. The prices of these foods, which drogpas are used to eating, have skyrocketed. They have to pay six to eight renminbi for one gyama(Approximately 500 gram) of milk and thirteen to fifteen renminbi for one gyama of meat. Drogpas have no choice but to wait – their throats dry and hands empty – for the compensation money the state provides them. Their previous independent source of living has now disappeared.

Loss of unity and solidarity

It is generally said that Tibetan people are kind and compassionate. Tibetan drogpas, in particular, have developed a harmonious relation with their surrounding environment, including the snow-mountains. Because of difficult travel and communication systems and other environmental hazards on the roof of the world, drogpas have had to settle in particular areas. In some places, only one or two families can be found. Cities with vast population have never existed. Drogpas are divided into different villages. When they migrate to greener pastures, treat animals infected with diseases and shear them for wool, drogpas seek the help of fellow drogpas from other villages. As a result, they get plenty of opportunities to mingle and cooperate with each other. Their experience of helping each other means drogpas have developed a culture of unity and solidarity among themselves.

With the resettlement in urban areas, drogpas have been deprived of work requiring collective efforts. They now abhor helping each other. Because of atomised lives, drogpa culture of unity and solidarity is disappearing. Without any cooperative interaction among themselves, drogpas remain isolated in their [concrete houses] staring blankly at each other.

Loss of culture of decency and respect

Tibetans are known to be decent people. To elders we accord the respect generally due to our parents. Those who are younger than us, we shower them with love and kindness as if they are our real siblings. More admirable than this is the kind of hospitality given to guests visiting our homes. Even beggars who possess nothing would be showered with clothes to wear and food to eat when they arrive in nomadic areas. When guests leave our homes, we have a beautiful culture of not walking in front or behind them. With the resettlement of dropgas in urban areas – in concrete houses – the culture of decency and respect among drogpas is disappearing. Drogpas now avoid visiting their neighbours. When they leave their houses, they put huge locks on their doors. They live their lives suspecting about anything that they see and touch. Their previous culture of hospitality, of inviting guests to their homes, has disappeared.

Loss of a unique livelihood

In the course of their long history, nations have developed their own unique source of livelihood. Tibetans are no exception. Drogpas have developed their own four-squared black tents to live in, three-headed hearths to light their homes, ropes to tie animals – thus crafting a livelihood autonomous and self-sufficient. Because of the creative genius of our ancestors, we have a unique dwelling called nomadic tent. These tents are constructed in such a way that they can absorb fresh air from outside, while getting rid of the damp air inside. The tents have the ability to keep dwellers warm during winter and cool during summer. Yak dung can easily catch fire in the three-headed hearths, causing no serious problems to nomads and their animals. Moreover, the art of weaving clothes give drogpas a good physical exercise. Whether milking their animals or churning out butter and cheese, such activities give them a good source of living and strong physique. Drogpa livelihood is thus unique and productive. With the resettlement of drogpas in urban areas, this unique livelihood is now disappearing. Unlike their drogpa ancestors, the coming generation shall be deprived of [the joy] of erecting tents, building hearths, milking animals and churning out butter and cheese.

Loss of ancestral homelands

Since ancient times, drogpas and their ancestors have been dwelling on high mountains blessed with pure rivers. Our ancestors have been performing the ritual of burning incense (sang) on mountains, throwing blessed mani stones (deu bum) into rivers, putting up prayer flags on the hills and hanging prayer flags on trees in forests. All these rituals, conducted for thousands of years, are meant to protect rivers, forests and mountains from pollution. We believe that digging out the earth will invite the wrath of nyens (evil spirits), polluting waters that of lu (nagas) and destroying mountains would alienate ancestral gods dwelling in them. Such myths and beliefs have served to protect Tibet's environment. Resettling the nomads haphazardly in urban areas by forcing them to sell their animals, all in the name of grassland protection means they will be displaced from their ancestral homelands. This will not work. An example could be given of Australia, a nation that relies heavily on animal husbandry. Australian government tried to increase the population of livestock by hunting down foxes. This, however, had a devastating impact on the population of livestock. In the end, the government was forced to bring foxes from other countries and released them on the grasslands. Similarly, there has to be an interdependent existence between livestock and grasslands of Tibet. Simply dispensing with the animals cannot

97

save Tibetan grasslands.

Just before this report goes to press, UNESCO will hear an application from the Chinese government to confer UNESCO World Heritage status for a vast area in Tibet of lakes, wetlands and wildlife from July 2, 2017.[63] Spreading over 60,000 km² area, known as Achen Gangyap in Tibetan and Hoh Xil, or Kekexili in Chinese, is in the middle of three major nature reserves that increasingly exclude normal Tibetan land use such as nomadic herding, situate the state as the sole agency of control, and encourage mass domestic tourism.

This plan, if approved by UNESCO will erode Tibet's fragile sources of rivers as it involves the removal and relocation of Tibetan nomads, who for centuries have managed to protect the environment, the grassland, its wildlife and the rivers which sustain them all.[64]

With its huge potential to develop into a profitable site for mass domestic tourism, this will reinforce China's plan to meet its official target to increase the number of annual domestic visits to Tibet to reach 20 million Chinese tourists by the year 2020 in the hope many of these tourists will settle in these areas.[65] This will lead to dramatic change in demographic composition of Tibet.

This raises serious concerns about China's nomination of Achen Gangyap for World Heritage Site. If UNESCO approves this nomination, it excludes herders and Tibetan nomads and it threatens the region's biodiversity. Such concerns were included in findings of a scientific evaluation team that travelled to Achen Gangyap in 2016 to carry out an official mission for UNESCO.[66] The delegation admitted that people had expressed concern to them about relocations. In a party-state that is found to be one of the least free countries in the world by Freedom House, their concerns must be taken into serious consideration as UNESCO sits to decide the fate of Tibetan nomads and their distinct culture. This must be seen in the light of other policies implemented in Tibet that further marginalize Tibetans in their own land.

Population Transfer and Western China 'Development' Programme

According to Jung Chang and Jon Halliday in their book, *Mao: the Unknown Story*, "From the time he conquered China, Mao was determined to take Tibet by force. When he saw Stalin on 22 January 1950, he asked if the Soviet air force could transport supplies to Chinese troops 'currently preparing for an attack on Tibet.' Stalin's reply was: 'It's good that you are preparing to attack. The Tibetans need to be subdued... 'Stalin also advised flooding Tibet and other border regions with Han Chinese: 'Since ethnic Chinese make up no more than 5 per cent of Xinjiang's population, the percentage of ethnic Chinese should be brought to 30... In fact, all the border territories should be populated by Chinese...' This is exactly what the Chinese communist regime then proceeded to do."[1]

In 1952, three years after founding the People's Republic of China, Mao Zedong said, "Tibet covers a large area but is thinly populated. Its population should be increased from the present two or three million to five or six million, and then to over ten million."[2] At that time Tibet had just been occupied by the Chinese communists in 1951 and yet Mao already had fully formed idea to swamp Tibet with Chinese.

In 1955, Liu Shaoqi, the president of the newly formed republic, told the late Panchen Lama that Tibet was a vast and thinly populated country and China had a big population which could be settled there.[3] In August 1957, Zhou Enlai, the Chinese premier, gave an important speech on the incorporation of non-Chinese regions into the national plan. The premier pointed out the shortage of land and underground natural resources in the Chinese-inhabited regions and the importance of developing natural resources in areas populated by the 'fraternal minority nationalities' to support the industrialization. Zhou said that the natural resources in the minority regions had been left untapped because of lack of labour power and technological expertise. The Chinese premier said, "Without mutual assistance, especially assistance from the Han people, the minority people will find it difficult to make significant progress on their own."

With clear guidelines from the highest leaders of the Communist Party, the *xiafang* campaign was launched in 1956. *Xiafang* or the 'downward transfer to the countryside' was a campaign to move millions of people from the urban areas of eastern China to the remote and sparsely-populated regions in the north and west with intention to integrate and assimilate the minorities. Over 600,000 people were sent to Amdo, Gansu, Ningxia, East Turkestan and Inner Mongolia in the first couple years after the campaign was launched.[4] A large number of Chinese also arrived in central Tibet.

Xiafang campaign was intensified during the Great Leap Forward, which produced disastrous consequences. The Great Leap Forward, launched in 1958, was a campaign to mobilize the masses to intensify China's economic growth. The result was a famine of such magnitude, unprecedented in China's own famine-stricken history. Scholars say about 20-30 million people died.[5] Others put the figure much higher.

After Deng Xiaoping came to powering 1978, he initiated the 'four modernizations' to revive China's stagnant economy. As a part of his 'four modernizations' drive Deng said in 1987 in regard to Tibet, "Tibet is sparsely populated. Two million Tibetans are not enough to handle the task of developing such a huge region. There is no harm in sending Han into Tibet to help... and move ahead in the four modernizations in China."[6] As part of his 'four modernizations' drive, Deng also demolished the commune system and let peasants have the right to private ownership of wealth. This led to an increased agricultural output, which in turn produced huge surplus in rural labour — the floating population. Millions of peasants, freed from the commune system, and unable to find jobs on their own in the rural areas because of increased mechanization of agriculture, drifted to urban China. Seeing such an exodus into cities as a threat to social stability, the Chinese authorities planned a step-by-step migration to the border regions of Xinjiang, Gansu and Tibet, including Tibetan areas in Gansu, Qinghai, Yunnan and

Sichuan. It was estimated that this vast region could absorb more than 100 million migrant Chinese workers.[7] These Chinese workers did indeed flock to sparsely-populated Tibet, to Tibetan urban areas like Lhasa, Shigatse, Chamdo and Gormo and urban centres in eastern and north-eastern Tibet.

According to *Tibet Under Communist China: 50 Years*, the Chinese population transfer to the TAR was carried out in earnest in the 1980s when Beijing launched the campaign to 'Help Tibet Prosper'. In May 1984 Radio Beijing reported that, "Over 60,000 workers, representing the vanguard groups to help in the construction work in the TAR, are arriving in Tibet daily and have started their preliminary work. They will be helping in the electricity department, schools, hotels, cultural institutions and construction of mills and factories."[8] Another 60,000 Chinese workers – mainly from Sichuan province – arrived in the TAR in the summer of 1985.[9] In the same year, there were 50,000 to 60,000 Chinese civilian residents in Lhasa alone, and within three years this figure doubled.[10]

The influx of Chinese settlers onto the Tibetan plateau accelerated in the early 1990s due to Deng Xiaoping's personal encouragement of the migration of large numbers of Chinese 'comrades' into Tibet to 'impart scientific and technological know-how and share their scientific expertise.'[11] In January 1991, *Beijing Review* reported that about 300,000 workers were prepared to join the new construction projects in the TAR.[12] In Lhoka alone about 28,000 Chinese settlers arrived between 1987 and 1992. 43,860 arrived in Nagchu between 1986 and 1992.[13]

Around this time Mao Rubai, vice-chairman of the TAR government was quoted as saying that apart from the PLA soldiers and other military personnel stationed in the autonomous region there were one million new Chinese settlers in the TAR.[14]

Tibet Under Communist China: 50 Years says it is the fertile Tibetan areas outside of the TAR'which have the highest concentration of Chinese migrants. These territories include the whole of Amdo and a substantial portion of Kham. Official Chinese statistics published between 1990 and 1995 show the total population of these regions as 7,742,000. Out of this Tibetans constituted 2,546,500, about 32.89 percent.[15]

Under various guises such as 'reducing the gap between the eastern provinces and western regions' and maintenance of 'sustained, stable and coordinated growth', population transfer was carried out. In 1992, Chen Kuiyuan, the party boss of TAR, even advocated setting up a framework which would allow and encourage extensive Chinese migration.

Chen said, "We should open Tibet wider to the outside. In other words, we should open Tibet to all countries and regions and open our job market to all fellow countrymen."[16]

Around this time, development programmes in Tibet emerged such as the plan to turn Lhasa-Shigatse-Tsethang triangle into a 'bread basket.' Elsewhere in TAR and other Tibetan areas, mining, logging of trees and commercial animal husbandry (to raise pigs, ducks and chickens to meet the demand of Chinese settlers in Tibet) were intensified. These economic projects and initiatives were further stepped up after the Third Work Forum on Tibet in 1994, which ushered in economically liberal but politically hard-line policies to assimilate Tibet in the Chinese economic, social and culture mainstream. The major thrust of the strategy was "to open Tibet's door wide to inner parts of the country and encourage traders, investments, economic units and individuals from China to central Tibet to run different sorts of enterprises."[17]

Massive highway constructions in Tibet and other infrastructural projects like the construction of airports, dams and extensive mining encouraged unskilled labourers from neighbouring provinces like Sichuan to flock into Tibet and transforming Tibetan cities and urban centres into so many Chinatowns.[18]

This influx of Chinese migrant workers made commodities in short supply and prices shot up. Pressure on the land and Tibetans became so apparent that a high-level Tibetan in TAR, remarked in 1992, "There is a little door and a big door. The little door opens to the outside world, and the big door opens to China ...The big door will outweigh the little door, and Tibet is more than ever in danger of being engulfed."[19]

Population transfer and resource extraction was expedited with the completion of the Lhasa-Gormo railway line in 2006. *Tracking the Still Dragon*, a report by the Washington, DC-based International Campaign for Tibet, says the railway line "has had a dramatic impact on the lives of Tibetans and on the land itself. As the 'centrepiece' and most visible symbol of Beijing's plan to develop the western regions of the People's Republic of China, the rail road is accelerating the influx of Chinese people to the plateau, exacerbating the economic marginalisation of Tibetans, and threatening Tibet's fragile high-altitude environment."[20]

During its first year Lhasa-Gormo railroad transported "1.5 million passengers into Tibet."[21] The director of TAR's Development and Reform Committee, Jin Shixun, stated that over 60 percent of the people coming into Tibet by train were businessmen, students and transient workers and only 40 percent were tourists.

However, according to *Tracking the Still Dragon*, "In 2006 a total of 2.51 million tourists visited TAR, almost matching the reported 2.7 million Tibetan residents in the whole of TAR, and this figure is expected to more than double by 2010."[22]

Such mass migration into isolated regions after railroad construction follows a pattern seen elsewhere in China. For instance, the Chinese population of Inner Mongolia increased five-fold after the completion of a railroad from Zhangjiakou in Hebei province to Hohhot, the capital city of Inner Mongolia from 1912 to 1949. By 1949 Chinese outnumbered the Mongolians 11 to one.

China exporting its excess population to the minority regions in the west and importing the region's vast and abundant natural resources was first formulated in China's seventh five-year plan (1986-1991).

103

Angela Knowx in her forward to *The Poverty of Plenty*, a book authored by Wang Xiaoqiang and Bai Nanfeng, writes, "Based on a model of regional comparative advantage, the plan sees the western regions as the providers of energy and mineral resources, to be used by the central provinces where much of China's energy and defence industry is based, the argument being that the wealth created in this region can later be shared with the west. The plan also provides personnel to be transferred from the east to the west in order to raise the level of technology there...In April 1988 the then party secretary Zhao Ziyang stated, 'Our goal is to seek common prosperity for all nationalities, but this cannot be achieved simultaneously.' For the time being, he said, the west was to supply the raw materials for the development of the east, and in return provide a ready market for the goods the east produces. Raising incomes, increasing marketization and exploiting natural resources in the west are clearly of major importance for this strategy."[23]

In fact, in their book, *The Poverty of Plenty*, Wang Xiaoqiang and Bai Nanfeng recommended that the central government create the infrastructures needed to exploit the natural resources of Tibet, East Turkestan (Ch. Xinjiang) and Inner Mongolia to feed the industries of coastal China. They also recommended that in these minority regions urban centres be established to house the Chinese migrant workers involved in resource extraction. This they hinted would serve the double purpose of relieving population pressure in China proper and establishing a growing Chinese presence in the minority regions that would serve to stifle separatist trends. This is China's master plan for the minorities: use the natural resources of minority regions to fuel China proper's economic development while pressing down the minorities by exporting China's excess population to these regions.[24]

More than a decade later, China came up with an overall solution to the pressing problems first articulated by Wang and Bai in *The Poverty of Plenty*. According to the London-based Tibet Information Network's publication, *China's Great Leap West*, "President Jiang Zemin launched the Western China Development Programme in a speech he gave in Xian on 17 June 1999. The initial emphasis of the campaign was on the acceleration of development focusing on the western regions, Tibet, which include Tibetan areas outside the autonomous region, Xinjiang, Sichuan, Gansu, Yunnan, Shaanxi, Ningxia, Guizhou and the Chongqing municipality, which altogether cover 56 per cent of China's total land mass and 23 percent of its total population. Party speeches on the subject were little more than lists of ideals and grand plans, devoid of context on implementation or priorities."[25]

Despite the vagueness of the economic priorities of the Western China Development Programme in the initial announcement, its political compulsions were clearly articulated right from the beginning. Party leaders have explicitly linked the success of the campaign to the survival of the party. Jiang Zemin, the then president of China, has been quoted as saying that the campaign "has major significance for the future prosperity of the country and the (Party's) long reign and perennial stability."[26] On 18 September 2000, Jiang Zemin was quoted by *China Daily*, as saying that developing the west "will help develop China's economy, stabilise local society and contribute to China's unity."[27]

But external developments also forced China to speed up the pace of the implementation of its Western China Development Programme. NATO military intervention in the war in Kosovo was perceived by the nervous regime in Beijing as a dangerous precedent set by the West for interference in a nation's internal affairs. Hu Angang, an economist at the Chinese Academy of Sciences, said, "The worst case scenario – and what we are trying to avoid – is China fragmenting like Yugoslavia... Already, regional (economic) disparity is equal to – or worse than – what we saw in Yugoslavia before it split."[28]

A Chinese economist living in the West, quoted in *China's Great Leap West*, explained it all when he said, "First of all the Chinese authorities are looking at the economic aspect, the western areas are very poor, and the standard of living needs to be increased. But Beijing is also concerned about the potential for social unrest, due to poverty and nationalistic feelings in areas such as Tibet and Xinjiang. Their real fear is that the west could become another Chechnya. That is the origin of the campaign to develop the west."[29]

So the solution China came up to solve its pressing political and economic problems in Tibet and elsewhere in the western region was the Western China Development Programme. Hidden behind this facade are the colonial power's greed for native resources and its need to control and extinguish native restlessness so as to facilitate Beijing's continued exploitation of native resources. Much of the "development" in the Western China Development Programme consists of construction of infrastructure: building of roads, laying of railway lines, airports and communication facilities, all geared towards facilitating the exploitation of the region's abundant natural resources and transporting these to China's resource-hungry coastal seaboard.

It is this aspect of the Western China Development Programme that is worrying Tibetans on the plateau. A Tibetan living in Lhasa summed up some of the deeper fears of the development of the west when he told Tibet Information Network, "The western development project aims to transfer large numbers of Chinese for permanent settlement into areas inhabited by minority nationalities, exploit mineral resources, and above all to bear down heavily on people for perceived political intransigence. Contrary to the claims of 'rare opportunity' for the minority nationalities, this campaign represents a period of emergency and darkness."

Thus contrary to the officially-expressed benign intentions of the Western China Development Programme, the real reasons and compulsions that are forcing the Chinese authorities to develop this vast, troublesome region is to ensure that the forces of market economy will succeed in fully integrating its 'Wild West' into China proper.

As a part of its Western China Development Programme, China came up with a number of projects to help migration of the poor or displaced Chinese population to Tibet. One of them was the Western Poverty Reduction Project. A component of this project is to develop agriculture in the Dulan area of Amdo and to relocate 58,000 Chinese settlers there. In 2000 the World Bank withdrew its US$40 million loan to this project in the face of protests from Tibetans and their international supporters. China said it would go ahead with the resettlement project using its own finance.[30]

In his book *Written in Blood*, the Tibetan author Tashi Rabten or Theurang writes that "each year the number of tourists [from China] increases ... and there are clear signs that a huge number of them are preparing themselves to settle in Tibet."[31]

The impact of this extraordinarily large influx of Chinese migrant workers into Tibet is multiple. The development in infrastructure to facilitate the extraction and transportation of Tibet's abundant and till now largely untapped natural resources is attracting increasing number of jobless Chinese workers to the TAR and other Tibetan areas. These Chinese workers benefit from government subsidies and an administration that favours them at the expense of Tibetans in terms of employment. Obtaining jobs often entails *guanxi*, "the backdoor" or connections with officials and a proficiency in Chinese language, which very few Tibetans have.[32] As a result, *Gongmeng Report* mentions that there is "a relentless trend of growing disparities" between Tibetan areas and Han areas and between urban and rural areas amid the process of rapid modernization and marketization.[33]

In order to accommodate this influx of Chinese settlers in Tibet, Beijing has initiated "massive construction schemes and rows upon rows of Chinese barrack-style housing"[34] which the authorities term as "a new highland city with national characteristics".[35] These uniform structures have appeared in most Tibetan towns and cities and are predominantly populated by fresh Chinese migrant workers and settlers.

In his essay *Tibet Through Chinese Eyes*, Peter Hessler, who travelled to Tibet, writes, "In Tibet Sichuanese have helped themselves to a large chunk of the economy. This was clear from the moment I arrived at the Lhasa airport, where thirteen of the sixteen restaurants bordering the entrance advertised Sichuan food. One was Tibetan. Virtually all small business in Lhasa follows this pattern; everywhere I saw Sichuan restaurants and shops. Locals told that 80 percent of Lhasa's Han were Sichuanese ... In front of the Jokhang, the holiest temple in Tibet, rows of stalls sell *khataks*, the ceremonial scarves that pilgrims use as offerings. It's a job one would expect to see filled by Tibetans [but] all the stalls were run by Sichuanese... There were more than 200 of them — relatives, friends of relatives, relatives of friends — and they had completely filled that niche."[36]

The influx of huge number of Chinese migrants, all with the same aim of making quick money, is eroding Tibetan cultural values and Tibet's environment. Perhaps, the worst impact is the everyday interactions that Tibetans have with this huge mass of migrant Chinese workers. Everyday, Tibetan values, traditional way of life and outlook to the world are gradually changing for the worse. The impact of this cultural invasion is reflected in changing habits, the decreasing use of Tibetan language and the new and much transformed urban landscape. These changes force Tibetans to adjust to the cultural influence of this "new majority" at the cost of Tibetan identity and culture.[37]

China's Urbancide in Tibet

The State Council of China unveiled the National New Type Urbanization Plan (NUP) in 2014 to increase the percentage of urban residents in the total population of China from 52.6 percent in 2012 to 60 percent by 2020. The ratio of citizens with urban *hukou* (resident permit) will increase 35.3 percent to approximately 45 percent. After many decades of deliberations and halt in reforms to the strict urban *hukou* system, the Chinese government has finally loosened procedures for rural migrants to transfer their household registrations to urban areas.

This policy has a unique impact on Tibet, where urbanization has become a major burden. Ethnically Chinese migrants coming from China's densely populated coastal provinces have started moving to Tibet and the reformed *hukou* system has made it easier to transfer their household registration in Tibet.

"Urbancide," refer to the extinguishing of Tibetan culture and identity through an influx of millions of Chinese migrants in Tibet. At the same time, Tibetans in rural regions are made landless through expropriation of their land. As suggested by Emily T. Yeh in her book, *Taming Tibet,* this is part of China's state territorialization of Tibet.[38]

According to James Leibold, senior lecturer in Chinese Politics and Asian Studies at La Trobe University in Melbourne argues that the Chinese state, as part of its arsenal of responses, has intensified urbanization, hoping that economic development and cultural contact will lead to assimilation and stability. [39]

The policy is already taking effect, as seen in the growth of Tibetan cities. As of 2016, Lhasa, Shigatse, Lhoka, Nyingtri, Tsoshar, Siling, and Chamdo were recognized as prefecture-level cities in Tibet. According to recent reports from China, two more will soon join that list: Nagchu and Ngari are to be upgraded from county-level cities to prefecture-level cities.

The late Bawa Phuntsok Wangyal, a high-ranking communist cadre in Tibet, pointed out in his book that cities should be centres of China's regional autonomous areas. Cities and towns of regional and national autonomous areas should have cultural, economic and political characteristics of people living in these areas. As a result of reforms and changes in these areas, in reality gradually these characteristics have disappeared and national and regional autonomy remains in name only. Majority of people living in these cities and town in Tibetan areas are Chinese migrants. This issue needs to be thought carefully and rectified.[40]

Hukou Reform: An Influx of Chinese Migrants in Tibet

Apart from government officials and military personnel who are transferred to Tibet, there has been a huge influx of ethnically Chinese migrants due to highly subsidized aid and investment in infrastructural development in Tibet. Chinese migrants, many of whom are facing a lack of employment opportunities in their home regions, are attracted to jobs and opportunities to start a business in Tibet. The population transfer from China to Tibet is following the same policy implemented in China-occupied Mongolia (today's Inner Mongolia) during the Qing Dynasty, where Mongolians were already a minority in the end of the 19th century. The agrarian focus of such policies meant that Chinese migrants settled in the countryside and they became dominant in rural as well as urban populations. The policy has continued through modern times: the number of cities in Inner Mongolia has increased from 193 in 1979 to 668 in 1997.[41]

The Western Region Development (WRD) Office of the State Council has suggested that no government authorities should collect urban population surcharge fees or similar fees from people moving their *hukous* to the Western Region.[42] This suggestion has further incentivized Chinese migrants to settle in Tibetan cities. In the coming decades, Tibet could witness a population growth of millions of Chinese migrants in various cities.

Rural Tibetans (Forced) Migration to Cities and Towns

Urbanization in Tibet has also encouraged many Tibetans living in rural areas to take up non-agricultural professions in Tibetan cities. Their ancestral lands are sold to land developers to build industries to attract migrants entering Tibet. As *Straits Times* reported recently, "Out of China's 31 provinces, regions, and municipalities, only the Tibet Autonomous Region (TAR) still maintains a distinction between rural and urban residents."[43] Because of the rural/urban classification scheme, Chinese migrants coming from outside Tibet are particularly encouraged to resettle in Tibetan cities, where they will have access to social welfare schemes.

In addition to natural migration patterns, a greater number of Tibetans from rural areas are being moved to towns through the government's forced resettlement policy. Pastoral Tibetans who live scattered with their herds in mountains and valleys are moved into compact and fenced residences. This allows the government to control the movement of these rural residents in the name of social stability. As Sophie Richardson, China director at the Human Rights Watch, pointed out, "Tibetans have no say in the design of [relocation] policies that are radically altering their way of life, and – in an already highly repressive context – no ways to challenge them." Rights violations during this process range from lack of consultation to failure to provide adequate compensation, both of which are required under international law for evictions to be legitimate. After the move, the sudden shift from nomadic life to cities has increased unemployment in Tibet.

A field study conducted by Tibetan researcher Gongbo Tashi (Alias Gonpo Tashi) and Marc Foggin in 2009 shows the empirical impact of ecological resettlement in Lhoka prefecture. The researchers interviewed more than 300 individuals in this survey. They found that forced resettlement deprived the residents of Dekyi village of their livestock, which was the main source of their livelihood. The new town where the villagers were resettled provided insufficient space to rear livestock. New farm training is supposed to be given to the resettled Tibetans to help them begin their new lives but most

Table No.1 Average livestock number, pre-resettlement in Dekyi village, Tsona county, Lhoka prefecture

Original County	Yak and Cattle		SHeep and Goats		Donkey and Horses	
	Before	After	Before	After	Before	After
Darnang county	1,320	255	876	107	267	0
Tsona county	2,457	126	1,260	32	253	0

n=42 households (over 300 individuals)
Source: Gonpo Tashi, 2009 survey

of the families complain about not receiving any of the training promised by the government before resettlement. As a result, the size of their livestock decreased dramatically, thereby making previously self-sufficient rural Tibetans heavily dependent on government subsidies. The table below indicates the shrinking size of livestock populations in Dekyi village after the resettlement [44]

Another experience of residents in two resettlements in Qinghai province from 2005-2009 could be taken as a case study. Residents were interviewed by a Chinese researcher, Xu Jun, with a group of other researchers. The group spent one month in each year in Yushul and Gormo prefecture in Amdo. In his study of these prefectures, where resettlement took place, Xu concluded that resettled nomads faced an intense sense of displacement: "We saw first-hand their struggle to make a new life as they resettle in a new place, puzzling over their future. Some are disappointed. Some are shameful, as they talked about their lives and having to rely on their relatives who remained in grassland. Some have to return to grassland to do some odd job to earn a living for their children." This five-year investigation showed that most of those resettled in or near cities during the period of the San Jiang Yun(Three parallel rivers project) protection and rebuilding program have not been able to make a living without access to grassland resources. On the other hand, no clear data exists to prove that such immigration had been helpful to the grassland ecosystem, which is the stated motive behind the relocations.[45]

Urbanization and Social Stability

In cities, unlike in remote areas of Tibet, people's movements and contacts can be monitored through a grid system. China carried out its first urban grid management experiment in Dongcheng district in Beijing in October 2004. [46] Down the road, if China remains devoid of real democratic checks and balances, there is little doubt that the continued development of grid management will only lead to a model for a modern police state in Tibet. This in part lends confidence to President Xi Jinping and Premier Li Keqiang's urbanization plan.

Human Rights Watch released a comprehensive report in 2013 [47] on how the urban grid management system in Lhasa, the capital of Tibet, has proven to be efficient in monitoring the movement of residents. In this new grassroots-level of urban administration, each "neighborhood" or "community" in towns will be divided into three or more grid units. At least eight pilot units were set up in Lhasa in April 2012, and in September they were declared to have "achieved notable results." In October of the same year, the regional party secretary stated that because "the Lhasa practice has fully proved the effectiveness of implementing grid management to strengthen and innovate social management [i.e., controlling mass protests]," the system should be made universal in "the towns, rural areas, and temples" of the TAR.

Land Expropriation

Nearby towns and remote villages in Tibet are now connected to

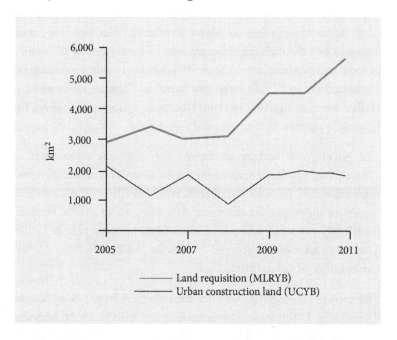

Sources: China Ministry of Land and Resources Yearbook, China Ministry of Housing and Rural - Urban Developments

113

extended cities. Land originally used for cultivation is increasingly seeing construction of vast infrastructure projects as well as residential and commercial buildings. According to the World Bank, rural land requisition and conversion for industrial use in China has been particularly inefficient because the decisions have been largely driven by administrative decisions rather than market demand [48]

China's urbanization has consumed significant land resources as urban boundaries are continuously expanding outward and the territorial jurisdictions of cities are increasing, primarily through the expropriation of surrounding rural land and its integration into urban areas. As indicated in the graph below, the demand for urban requisition of land has soared over the past few years in China due to the urbanization project.

Between 2001 and 2011, the amount of land in China classified as urban construction land had increased by 17,600 square kilometers (sq km), reaching a total area of 41,805 sq km in 2011, an increase of 58 percent over a decade. About 90 percent of demand for urban land was met through the expropriation of rural land, while only 10 percent was supplied from the existing stock of undeveloped urban construction land. Following this trend, as Tibetan cities grow, a sizable amount of rural land in Tibet will be expropriated by the Chinese government.

The government and, to an extent, the academic community in China, have largely overlooked the implication of rapid urbanization for millions of farmers or villagers who have been made landless (legally or illegally) over the years. According to an official statistic, three million people become landless farmers every year in China. The total number is expected to double in 2020 because of the current pace of urbanization.[49]

The growth of cities has another consequence. In her book *Taming Tibet,* Emily T. Yeh stated that according to China's Law of Regional National Autonomy (LRNA), when regions, prefectures, and counties are upgraded to cities, the autonomous status of these areas will be lost. Uradyn Bulag, an anthropologist who researches Inner Mongolia, advanced the argument that the benefits of an administrative promotion from county to city, particularly for local leaders, "checkmates ethnic sensitivity" about the loss of ethnic autonomous status.

China's urbanization in Tibet (and across the country) is aimed as a solution to China's slowing economy. The policy is intended to bring millions of Chinese migrant workers to settle and do business in Tibet. As part of this process, Tibet's cities have gone through demographic shifts, resulting in the strong influence of Chinese culture.

The projected rate of 30 percent urbanization in Tibet in the coming few decades would mean that all cities in Tibet will be dominated by ethnic Chinese. As a result, Tibetans lose the language rights associated with autonomous status. Meanwhile, mobility and communication for urban residents is monitored strictly whenever the government deems it necessary.

To feed the growth of cities, land, which is the only asset that many rural Tibetans inherit from their ancestors, is bought by state-owned enterprises (SOEs) and foreign companies. Tibetans from rural areas who lose their land must look for unskilled, usually temporary work. If the current rate of urban land requisition by the Chinese government continues, the ownership of land in many areas in Tibet will be transferred to Chinese migrants, businesses, and the state.

In response to these changes, Tibetan resistance will grow stronger. Urbanization in Tibet, with the resulting damage to traditional ways of life, cannot win the hearts of Tibetans as explicitly called for by Xi Jinping at the last Work Forum[50] held in Tibet. It has only created more resentment among Tibetans.

Tibet Under Communist China: 50 Years sums up China's rule in Tibet in the following words, "Earlier communist China looked at Tibet more from a geopolitical and security perspective. Now coupled with this enduring imperial reason for staying put in Tibet, an economically vibrant China looks to Tibet as the best source for coastal China's galloping demand for energy, fuel and water. The devastating impact of this change in attitude toward Tibet is already felt in Tibet as Tibetans, unable to compete with more skilled Chinese settlers, are increasingly marginalised by the forces of globalisation unleashed on the roof of the world. Having lost their country, Tibetans in increasing number are losing their jobs and their future to the Chinese settlers streaming to Tibet to take advantage of the economic boom."[51]

Mining Tibet - Mineral Exploitation in Tibetan Areas of the PRC, a report by the London-based Tibet Information Network, published in 2002, says, "Many Tibetans see the immigration of large numbers of Chinese into Tibetan areas as the most serious threat to their land and resources and to traditional Tibetan livelihoods and culture."[52]

"I do not see we have that long before we reach the point of no return. I am not saying all Tibetans are going to disappear but by then there will be so many Chinese in Tibet, it will be no longer realistic for the Tibetan people to regain a Tibet for Tibetans. What has happened to the native Americans, to the native Australians, is happening in Tibet,"[53] Lhasang Tsering, a Tibetan writer and activist, says in *The Sun Behind the Cloud*, a documentary on the Tibetan struggle for freedom by Ritu Sarin and Tenzing Sonam, two veteran filmmakers.

Given these fears, it is only natural for Tibetans to suspect, as many do in Tibet, that China wants Tibet and not the Tibetans.

Conclusion

An estimated 2.25 million nomads live on the Tibetan Plateau. For ages the Tibetan nomads skilfully managed their livestock and sustained the land while adapting to the realities of Tibet's fragile ecological system. Since 2002, the Chinese government has been implementing forced resettlement, land confiscation, and fencing policies in pastoral areas inhabited primarily by Tibetans, drastically curtailing their livelihood. Herders have been required to slaughter or sell off their livestock and move into newly-built housing colonies, abandoning their traditional way of life.

Over 700,000 nomads have been settled since 2000 and the official Chinese media state that 1.32 million Tibetan nomads will have settled within a few years. The relocation in permanent settlements has severed their intimate connection with their animals, and rendered their knowledge of animal and grassland management, inherited from one generation to another, useless.

In December 2010 the UN Special Rapporteur on the right to food, Olivier De Schutter, has encouraged the Chinese authorities to reassess its nomad removal policies stating that it "leaves the nomads with no other options than to sell their herd and resettle." However, Beijing's forceful removal of Tibetan nomads from traditional pastoral lives goes on, thus destroying over 9000 years of Tibet's mobile civilization.

China's final solution to Tibetan culture and way of life is its policy of population transfer into Tibet. This began with *xiafang* or the 'downward transfer to the countryside' launched in 1956. This was a campaign to move millions of Chinese from the urban areas of eastern China to the remote and sparsely-populated regions such as Tibet with intention to integrate and assimilate the minorities. Over 600,000 people were sent to Amdo, East Turkestan and Inner Mongolia in the first couple years after the campaign was launched.

The campaign was intensified during the Great Leap Forward, which resulted in a famine of such magnitude, unprecedented in China's own famine-stricken history. Scholars say over 30 million people died.

During Deng's 'four modernizations' campaign, more Chinese were encouraged to go to sparsely populated Tibet. Millions of peasants, freed from the commune system, and unable to find jobs on their own in the rural areas because of increased mechanization of agriculture, drifted to urban China. Seeing such an exodus into cities as a threat to social stability, the Chinese authorities planned a step-by-step migration to the border regions like Tibet and East

Turkestan. It was estimated that this vast region could absorb more than 100 million migrant Chinese workers. In 1984, there were 50,000 to 60,000 Chinese civilian residents in Lhasa alone, and within three years this figure doubled.

Population transfer and resource extraction was expedited with the completion of the Lhasa-Gormo railway line in 2006, which transported 1.5 million passengers into Tibet in that year alone. Over 60 percent of the people coming into Tibet by train were businessmen, students and transient workers and only 40 percent were tourists. Such mass migration into isolated regions after railroad construction follows a pattern seen in Inner Mongolia after the completion of a railroad to Hohhot, the capital city of Inner Mongolia in 1911. By 1949 Chinese outnumbered the Mongolians 11 to one.

The impact of the population transfer through the *xiafang* campaign, the railroad and the Western Development Program represents a period of emergency for the Tibetans. This extraordinarily large influx of Chinese settlers in Tibet has multiple effects. The extraction and transportation of Tibet's abundant and till now untapped natural resources benefits the Chinese at the expense of Tibetans. The Chinese have also helped themselves to a large chunk of the economy such as restaurants, small businesses and government jobs.

However, the biggest blow is the erosion of Tibetan cultural values and Tibet's environment. The everyday interactions that Tibetans have with this huge mass of migrant Chinese workers change Tibetan values, traditional way of life and outlook to the world for the worse. This cultural invasion is reflected in changing habits, the decreasing use of Tibetan language and the new and much transformed urban landscape. These changes force Tibetans to adjust to the cultural influence of this "new majority" at the cost of Tibetan identity and culture.

Thus the combined impact of China's systematic destruction of Tibetan religion, distortion and damage on Tibetan education and language, forceful removal of nomads, and the population transfer policy is the complete annihilation of the Tibetan culture and way of life. These may keep the Tibetans physically intact, but the collective Tibetan identity suffers in a fundamental and irremediable manner. This is cultural genocide in intent and in deed.

Recommendations

- That Tibet under China is a stark reminder to the rest of the world that there is an urgent need to further develop Raphael Lemkin's concept of cultural genocide and to include this in international law

- That this report should serve as a basis for scholars, researchers and concerned institutions to conduct further systematic academic study and research on Tibet and other similar cases around the world by holding frequent seminars and conferences on the subject of cultural genocide and to be allowed to do field research

- That the world leaders and the international community must and should take proactive stand regarding the cultural genocide that is taking place in Tibet

- That the Chinese government should cease all policies leading to systematic destruction of Tibetan and stop the party's daily dictates on 'correct' thinking

- That the Tibetans should have full freedom to inherit and creatively develop their traditional culture and religion

- That the media, scholars, environmentalists and researchers should actively seek access to Tibet and the Tibetans to report about the ongoing cultural genocide in Tibet which could make valuable contribution to overall debates and discussions on "cultural genocide" as Lemkin defined and as was included in the draft 1947 UN Genocide Convention

** end ***

NOTES

Destruction Documented by Scholars, Jurists and the UN

1 *So Close to Heaven – The Vanishing Buddhist Kingdoms of the Himalayas* by Barbara Crossette. p. xii

2 see *A Cultural History of Tibet* by David Snellgrove and Hugh Richardson

3 ibid

4 see *The Question of Tibet and the Rule of Law* by International Commission of Jurists. 1959.

5 see *Tibet and the Chinese People's Republic: a report to the International Commission of Jurists by its Legal Inquiry Committee on Tibet.* 1960.

6 see *Tibet: Human Rights and the Rule of Law.* 1997

7 UN resolution no.1353 (ivx). 1959

8 UN resolution no.1723 (xvi). 1961

9 UN resolution no.2070 (xx). 1965

10 see *Situation in Tibet.* No. E/N.4/sub.2/91, 43 Session

11 see *Tibet: Human Rights and the Rule of Law.* 1997

12 ibid

13 ibid

Tibetan View on the Destruction: the 10th Panchen Lama and His Petition

1 *Namsa Gojey by Shogdung (The Line Between Sky and Earth)*. pp.72-74

2 *Tsenpoi Nyingtop (The Fierce Courage)* by Gartse Jigme. pp.44-45

3 ibid

4 *Surviving the Dragon* by Arjia Rinpoche. p.vii

5 Joint Statement of Lama Karma Tenzin in *Tibet Under Chinese Communist Rule: a compilation of refugee statements 1958-75.* p.116

6 ibid p.119

7 Statement of Yeshi Chophel in *Tibet Under Chinese Communist Rule: a compilation of refugee statements 1958-75.* p.122

8 Imprisonment. *My Life My Culture* by Dr Lobsang Wangyal. p.32

9 Chapter 2 of *Xi Zang Xing Shi He ren Wu Jiao Yu De Ji Ben Jiao Cai.*

Zhong guo ren min jei fang jun. xi zang jun qu zheng zhi bu bian yin. 1960 nian 10 yue 1 ri. p.6

10 see *Ping Xi Xizang Pan Luan. Xi zang ren min chu ban she. Xizang zizhi qu duang shi zi liao zhen ji wei yuan hui. Xizang jun qu dang shi zi liao zhengji lingdao xiao zhu.* p.34

11 Ngamda near Rivoche, Shopamdo near Lhorong, Tengchen and Lhari Dzong are currently in the 'TAR'. These are some of the important and strategically located towns along the route that the PLA troops took (in 1959-60) to reach Lhasa, Tibet's capital city.

12 see The Panchen Lama's Letter in *Hungry Ghosts: China's Secret Famine.* p.171

13 see Tibet Enslaved in *In Exile from the Land of Snow.* p.263

14 Chapter 9. The Sacred Tree and Time Machine in *Surviving the Dragon.* pp.137-38

15 as quoted in *Hu Yaobang's Visit to Tibet, May 22-31, 1980* by Wang Yao, in *Resistance and Reform in Tibet.* pp.287-88

16 for more on the protests see *Circle of Protest: Political Ritual in the Tibetan Uprising*

17 for more on the Third Work Forum on Tibet (1994) and its impact see *Cutting Off the Serpent's Head: Tightening Control in Tibet, 1994-1995;* and *Golden Bridge Leading to a New Era*

Why the Destruction?

1 for example Wang Yangming, during the Ming Dynasty (1386-1644), wrote: "barbarians were like animals. For Han officials to try to govern them through civil administration would be like a man trying to tame a pack of deer in his own living room," and that the only way to discipline them is "to split up the domains of the various chiefs means to establish zones of restriction and fits into the policy of circumcising stallions and castrating boars." For more see *Old Tibet a Hell on Earth? The Myth of Tibet and Tibetans in Chinese Art and Propaganda* by Thomas Heberer in *Imagining Tibet: perceptions, projections and fantasies.*

2 *The Argumentative Indian* by Amartya Sen. p.174

Chinese Communist Leaders' view on Tibetan Culture

1 *My Land and My People.* p.118

2 as quoted *The Struggle for Tibet.* p.166

3 *Dus Rabs Gsar par Skyod Pa'i Gser Zam (A Golden Bridge Leading to a New Era)* p.74

4 ibid p.66

5 as quoted in *Tibet – Human Rights and Rule of Law.* International Commission of Jurists. p. 109.

6 as quoted in TIN NEWS, Review No. 25 *Reports from Tibet* 1996

7 ibid

8 speech made at the 6th TAR Political Consultative Conference. 14 May 1996

9 speech made at the TAR Party Committee. 8 November 1997

10 as quoted in *The Struggle for Tibet.* p.175

11 Jiang's speech at the National Committee of the Chinese People's Political Consultative Conference Working Meeting on religious Affairs. 12 December 2001.

12 Speech by the then Vice-president Hu Jintao at the 50th anniversary of Tibet's 'liberation.' 19 July 2001. Available at: http://news.xinhuanet.com/english/20010719/431559.htm

13 ibid

14 see Kashag's (Cabinet of the Tibetan Government in Exile) speech on Tibetan Democracy Day. 2 September 2000.

15 *Interview with Tibet's Communist Party Chief.* Der Spiegel. 16 August 2006.

16 as quoted in *Al Jazeera.* Available at: *http://english.aljazeera.net/news/asia-pacific/2010/03/201031085048872552.html*

17 see *Facts About the 17-point "Agreement" Between Tibet and China.* DIIR. Dharamsala. 22 May 2001.

18 *Constitution of the People's Republic of China*

19 for more see *Religion in China Today* (edited by Donald MacInnis) in which the full document is reprinted. pp.8-26

20 *Circle of Protest – political ritual in the Tibetan uprising* by Ronald D. Schwartz in which the full document is reprinted. pp.235-43

21 *dus rabs gsar par skyod pa'i gser zam (A Golden Bridge Leading to a New Era).* A document issued after the Third Work Forum on Tibet was

held from 20-23 July 1994, which marked a clear move towards a hardline policy regarding Tibetan religion, culture and intellectual freedom. The First Work Forum was held in 1980, and the Second in 1984.

22 *Cutting Off the Serpent's Head,* in which the full document is printed, including those passages that were omitted from the public version. pp.150-68

23 the full document in Chinese is available at: www.sohu. com/20070802/n251386214.shtml

Although the document does not mentions Dalai Lama by name, it can be clearly inferred from "those [reincarnations] with a particularly great impact shall be reported to the State Council for approval" meaning that the highest authority in the PRC will interfere in the selection of the future Dalai Lama

24 full text of the *Order No. 2* or "Measures for dealing strictly with rebellious monasteries and individual monks and nuns" is available in *Tibet at a Turning Point: The Spring Uprising and China's New Crackdown.* pp.137-139

Eradication of Tibetan Buddhism

1 see *Introduction to a Contribution to the Critique of Hegel's Philosophy of Right* by Karl Marx

2 *Lenin Collected Works.* Progress Publishers. 1965. Moscow. Volume 10. p.83

3 see *My Land My People.* p.118

4 as quoted in *The Nationalities Policy of the CCP* by W. Smith in *Resistance and Reform in Tibet.* p.61

5 see *The Question of Tibet and the Rule of Law* by International Commission of Jurists. 1959.

6 *How the Swans Came to the Lake: A Narrative History of Buddhism in America.* p.276

7 *Mao: The Unknown Story.* p.556

8 personal correspondences with Arjia Rinpoche

9 *A Poisoned Arrow: The Secret Report of the 10th Panchen Lama.* p.9

10 ibid p.26

11 ibid p.55

12 ibid p.52

13 see *Buddha's Warrior.* p.165

14 ibid

15 *The end of Tibetan Buddhism* by Wang Lixiong in *The Struggle for Tibet.* pp.147-189

16 ibid

17 *Dragon In the Land of Snow.* pp.320-21

18 Ribhur Tulku as quoted in *CHINA's Tibet? Autonomy or Assimilation.* pp.127-130

19 *My Life My Culture.* p.45

20 *Dragon In the Land of Snow.* p.316

21 see *Tibet Under Communist China: 50 Years*; also see *Authenticating Tibet*

22 *Search for Jowo Mikyo Dorjee.* p.6

23 for more see *Memoirs of Keutsang Tulku.*

24 *Fire Under Snow: True Story of a Tibetan Monk.* pp.66-67

25 for more on DMC see *A Poison Arrow.* p.52; *Forbidden Freedom: Beijing's Control of religion in Tibet.* pp.24-30; and *Golden Bridge Leading to a New Era.* p.80

26 *Forbidden Freedom: Beijing's Control of Religion in Tibet.* p.26

27 *Golden Bridge Leading to New Era.* p.74

28 ibid p.80

29 ibid. pp65-67

30 *Xinhua News.* 30 June 2000

31 *Strike Hard" Campaign: China's Crackdown on Political Dissidence.* p.27. For more see *The Communist Party as Living Buddha: The Crisis Facing Tibetan Religion Under Chinese Control.* p.108

32 *Golden Bridge…* p.77

33 for more see *Tibet At a Turnign Point.* p.75

34 *Tibet Daily.* 18 April 2001.

35 for more on Larung Gar destruction and Khenpo Jigme Phuntsok see *Destruction of Serthar Institute : A special report. TCHRD. Available at:*

http://www.tchrd.org/publications/topical_reports/destruction_of_serthar-2002/ and Jigme Phuntsok: Buddhist monk whose settlement at Larung Gar in Tibet attracted thousands until it was brutally destroyed by the Chinese.

12 January 2004. Available at: *http://www.timesonline.co.uk/tol/comment/obituaries/article992925.ece*

36 for more on Tulku Tenzin Delek see *Trials of a Tibetan Monk: The Case of Tenzin Delek,* vol.16, no.1, February 2004. www.hrw.org/reports/2004/china204/index.htm. and *Unjust Sentence.* TCHRD available at

www.tchrd.org/publications/topical_reports/unjust_sentence-trulku_tenzin_delek-2004/trulku.pdf

37 *Annual Report 2009* by United States Commission on International Religious Freedom. p.75

38 see Congressional-Executive Commission on China. *2007 Annual Report;*

39 crackdown by the Chinese authorities has increased since 2008 not only on religious leaders but also on public intellectuals such as writers, singers and others who are involved in social services such as starting an orphanages etc. see *A Raging Storm: The Crackdown on Tibetan Writers and Artistes after Tibet's Spring 2008 Protests*

40 for more see *Colossal Guru Rinpoche's statue demolished in Tibet: China's new religious affairs regulations for ' TAR' entered into force.* TCHRD. June 2007. Available at: http://www.tchrd.org/publications/hr_updates/2007/hr200706.pdf and *Demolition giant Buddha statue at Tibetan monastery confirmed by China.* ITC. Available at:

http://www.savetibet.org/media-center/ict-news-reports/demolition-giant-buddha-statue-tibetan-monastery-confirmed-china

41 *Order No. Five* issued by the State Religious Affairs Bureau of PRC. 18 July 2007.

42 personal correspondences with Arjia Rinpoche

43 see *The End of Tibetan Buddhism* by Wang Lixiong in *The Struggle for Tibet.*

44 *An Investigative Report Into the Social and Economic Causes of the 3.14 Incident in Tibetan Areas. Gongmeng Law Research Center.*

45 ibid

46 *Golden Bridge...* p.75

47 Questions of the first term examination for the nuns of Tsamkhung Nunnery "in order to deepen the Patriotic Education." The test paper (2006) contains 30 questions on various issues such as

religion, politics and how to 'oppose the Dalai clique' etc.

48 *The "Strike Hard" Campaign: China's crackdown on political dissidence.* p.22

49 *Communist Party as Living Buddha.* p.107

50 *Tibet at a Turning Point: The Spring Uprising and China's New Crackdown.* p.75

51 ibid p.137

52 ibid p.88

53 ibid pp.137-38

54 ibid p.139

55 VOT radio broadcast. 23 July 2010. *www.vot.org*

56 *The Struggle for Tibet* pp.147-189

57 *Stick Out Your Tongue.* p.84

58 *A Poisoned Arrow.* p.105

59 see *Social Evils: Prostitution and Pornography in Tibet.* TIN. Also see Days of Debauchery in *Tibetan Bulletin.* January-April 2000. .

Damage and Distortion in Education and Tibetan Language

1 *Politicisation and the Tibetan Language* by Tsering Shakya in *Resistance and Reform.* p.159

2 *Education in Tibet: policy and practice since 1950.* p.20

3 *sum rtags mtha' dpyad las bod kyi spyi skad skor.* pp 17-34

4 *Life In the Red Flag People's Commune.* p.23

5 as quoted in *Education in Tibet.* p.38

6 ibid

7 ibid p.21

8 for more see *The Chinese Frontiersman and the Winter Worms – Chen Kuiyuan In the TAR, 1992-2000*

9 full text of the speech is available in *Education in Tibet.* pp.272-279

10 ibid

11 ibid

12 ibid

13

14 *Golden Bridge Leading to a New Era.* p.40

15 for more on this see *Education in Tibet.* pp 53-54; also see *China: Minority Exclusion, Marginalization and Rising Tension* by Human Rights

in China. p.29

16 a moderate estimate number of Tibetans who have escaped into exile is over 80,000 since the 1980s. About two to three thousand refugees come from Tibet each year. However, the number has dramatically reduced since 2008 due to strict border patrolling by the Chinese authorities.

17 see *Gongmeng Report* or *An Investigative Report into the Social and Economic Causes of the 3.14 Incident in Tibetan Areas.*

18 ibid

19 ibid

20 ibid

21 read *We Have Our Own Religious Symbols, Our Own Culture and History* by Woeser. Available at: www.highpeakspureearth.com/2010/02/we-have-our-own-religious-totems-our.html

22 ibid

23 *Tibet Through Chinese Eyes* (part 1, 2 & 3) by Peter Hessler published and available on *The Atlantic Online* www.theatlantic.com

24 see *Gongmeng Report*

25 ibid

26 *Trag-Yig* or *Written in Blood.* p.110

27 as quoted in *Tibet Under Communist China: 50 Years.* p.40

28 ibid p.41

29 ibid

30 *China: Minority Exclusion, Marginalization and Rising Tension* by Human Rights in China. pp.18-19

31 ibid pp.26-31

32 for more see *The Chinese Frontiersman and Winter Worm*

33 ibid

34 for more on Woeser see www.nytimes.com/2009/04/25/world/asia/25woeser.html

35 see http://www.pen.org/viewmedia.php/prmMID/1919/prmID/172

36 *A 'Raging Storm': The Crackdown on Tibetan and Artists After Tibet's Spring 2008 Protests*

37 ibid

38 ibid

39 ibid

40 see *Race Against Time to Save Manchu Language.* Available at: www.china.org.cn/english/culture/167537.htm Also see *Mustering the Strength to Save Manchu.* Available at: http://tyglobalist.org/index.php/20090105171/focus/Mustering-the-Strength-to-Save-Manchu.html

41 ibid

42 ibid

43 ibid

44 Tournadre. N. (2003). Roundtable before the Congressional executive commission on China on teaching and learning Tibetan: The role of Tibetan language in Tibet's future 7 April, 2003. Retrieved 23 June, 2017. http://www.cecc.gov/sites/chinacommission.house.gov/files/documents/roundtables/2003/CECC%20Roundtable%20Testimony%20-%20Nicolas%20Tournadre%20-%204.7.03.pdf

45 A few proposed suggestion by Jigme Gyaltsen, High Peak Pure Earth, 21 Febuary, 2010, http://highpeakspureearth.com/2014/a-few-proposed-suggestions-on-education-by-jigme-gyaltsen/(Accessed17, June 2017)

46 Report prepared by CTA (1995). The World-Wide Web Virtual Library. Retrieved June 2, 2017, from http://www.ciolek.com/WWVLPages/TibPages/TibetWomen-Exile.html

47 འབགར་རྗེ་འཇིགས་མེད། (༢༠༡༩) བཙན་པོའི་སྲིད་སྐྱོབས། ས་རུ་བོད་ཀྱི་དཔེ་སྐྲུན་ཁང་། ཤོག་གྲངས། (༦)

48 Bass.C. (1998) Education in Tibet Policy and Practie since 1950. (TIN) London and New York. Zed Books p.237. 240

49 "Students Protest Language Change," Radio Free Asia, 19 October, 2010, http://www.rfa.org/english/news/tibet/language-10192010170120.html (Accessed 20 June, 2017)

50 Protests by students against downgrading of Tibetan language spread to Beijing, ICT, 22 October 2010, https://www.savetibet.org/protests-by-students-against-downgrading-of-tibetan-language-spread-to-beijing/ Accessed 15 June, 2017)

51 Tibetans protest against language curbs in Chinese schools,

The Guardian, 20 October,2010, https://www.theguardian.com/world/2010/oct/20/tibetans-protest-language-chinese-schools (Accessed 21 June, 2017)
52 China: Drop Charges Against Tibetan Education Activist, Human Rights Watch, 15 January, 2017 https://www.hrw.org/news/2017/01/15/china-drop-charges-against-tibetan-education-activist (Accessed 28 June, 2017)
53 A Tibetan Journey for Justice, New York Times https://www.nytimes.com/video/world/asia/100000004031427/a-tibetans-journey-for-justice.html (Accessed 28 June, 2017)

The Destruction of the Nomadic Way of Life
1 as quoted in *The Nationalities Policy of the CCP* by Warren Smith in *Resistance and Reform*. p.65
2 ibid p.66
3 full text of *Communalization in a Single Stride* is available in *A Poisoned Arrow*. pp.161-163
4 ibid
5 ibid
6 *A Poisoned Arrow*. p.10
7 ibid p.110
8 for more see *Tibet Under Chinese Communist Rule: A Compilation of Refugee Statements 1958-1975*. p.119 and p.122
9 *A Poisoned Arrow*. p.30
10 *No One has the Liberty to Refuse*. p.17
11 ibid
12 *Northern Tibet Grassland Takes on a New Look*. 19 May 2009. Available at www.eng.tibet.cn/news/today/200905/t20090519_477226_1.htm.
13 for a detailed report on the traditional Tibetan environmental protection see *High Sanctuary, wildlife and nature conservatory in Old Tibet* by Norbu, Jamyang. 6 December 2009. Available at www.shadowtibet.com. Also see *Ecological Responsibility: a dialogue with Buddhism* edited by Julia Martin
14 *No One has the Liberty to Refuse*. p.3
15 ibid pp.3-4

16 ibid p.3

17 ibid p.27

18 as quoted in *No One has the Liberty to Refuse.* p.35

19 *Constructing a green railway on the Tibet Plateau: Evaluating the effectiveness of mitigation measure.* Available at www.elsevier.com/locate/trd

20 ibid

21 ibid

22 for more on this see *Mining in Tibet.* pp.77-114; *Tracking the Steel Dragon.* pp.61-72; *The Political Economy of Boomerang Aid in China's Tibet* by Andrew Fischer in *CHINA Perspective.* No. 2009/3

23 see *Perversities of Extreme Depdendence and Unequal Growth in TAR.* Tibet Watch Special Report August 2007.

24 *No One has the Liberty to Refuse.* pp.39-44

25 as quoted in *Politicisation and the Tibetan Language* by Warren Smith in *Resistance and Reform.* p.159

26 for a detailed report on the traditional Tibetan environmental protection see *High Sanctuary, wildlife and nature conservatory in Old Tibet* by Jamyang Norbu. 6 December 2009. Available at: www.shadowtibet.com; Also see *Ecological Responsibility: A Dialogue with Buddhism* edited by Julia Martin

27 Morton, Katherine. *Climate Change on the Tibetan Plateau: A New Security Challenge.* Woodrow Wilson Center. Washington DC. 12 February, 2009 available at: http://www.wilsoncenter.org/ondemand/index.cfm?fuseaction=Media.play&mediaid=A98B9EA0-B257-1FBB-7079F3FB8A24667F

28 see at http://chinatibet.people.com.cn/6829088.html

29 *Tibet to Bolster Agricultural, Animal Husbandry in 2009.* 11 February 2009. Available at: http://eng.tibet.cn/news/today/200902/t20090211_451880.htm.

30 *No One has the Liberty to Refuse.* pp.57-64

31 ibid p. 49; also see *The Struggle for Tibet.* pp.160-168; *Fungus gold rush in Tibetan plateau rebuilding lives after earthquake* by Jonathan Watts. 17 June 2010. The Guardian. Available at: http://www.guardian.co.uk/environment/2010/jun/17/fungus-tibetan-plateau

32 *Fungus gold rush in Tibetan plateau rebuilding lives after earthquake.* The Guardian. 17 June 2010.

33 *No One has the Liberty to Refuse.* pp.64-71

34 ibid p.69

35 see *Tibetan Nomads in a Fix?* By Anthony Kuhn. *Tibetan Bulletin.* July-September 2002.

36 *No One has the Liberty to Refuse.* pp.31-59

37 12 *Northern Tibet Grassland Takes on a New Look.* 19 May 2009. Available at: www.eng.tibet.cn/news/today/200905/t20090519_477226_1.htm.

38 for more see Drokpa in Peril; and Pastoral-Nomadism of Tibet: between Tradition and Modernization. *Tibetan Bulletin.* September-December. 2000

39 Census Office of the TAR, 2002, The 2000 Census Data of the TAR (Vol. 1), Beijing: Statistical Press of China. In Chinese; HRW 2013: 34

40 HRW 2013: 4

41 ibid

42. "Massive nomad settlement to protect 'mother river,'" The Global Times, 30 November 2012, http://www.globaltimes.cn/content/747536.shtml (Accessed 29 November, 2017)

43 "Tibet to invest 400 million yuan in nomad's settlement,"13 September, 2012, cctv.cn, http://english.cntv.cn/20120913/103363.shtml (Accessed 29 June, 2016)

44 Schutter , Olivier. Report of the Special Rapporteur on the right to food, Olivier

De Schutter- Mission to China. UN Human Rights Council, 2012

45 HRW 2013:4

46 Lai, Hongyi Harry (October 2002). "China's Western Development Program: Its Rationale, Implementation, and Prospects"Modern China. Sage Publications

47 ibid

48 Paul, Cheng 2011: 170-171

49 Information Office of the State Council of the People's Republic of China, "Fifty Year of Democratic Reform in China," unpublished document, March 2, 2009. http://www.china.org.cn/government/whitepaper/node_7062754.htm (Accessed 29 June, 2017)

50 HRW 2013: 40

51 ibid 41

52 "Tibet to achieve leapfrog development, lasting stability China Daily, "January 23, 2010, (accessed June 29, 2017), http://www.globaltimes.cn/content/500489.shtml

53 HRW 2013: 42

54 "Tibet to achieve leapfrog development, lasting stability China Daily, "January 23, 2010, (accessed June 29, 2017), http://www.globaltimes.cn/content/500489.shtml

55 "Nomadic people in Qinghai to settle within five years," People's Daily Online, March 11, 2009, (accessed June 29, 2017), http://en.people.cn/90001/90776/90882/6611715.html

56 HRW 2013:43

57 HRW 2013: 62-108

58 "Eight losses faced by Tibetan drogpas due to China's resettlement policy," TCHRD, (accessed June 26, 2017)

59 Andrew Fischer, State Growth and Social Exclusion in Tibet: Challenges of Recent Economic Growth, (Copenhagen: Nordic Institute of Asian Studies Press, 2005)

60 HRW 2013: 45

61Andrew M. Fisher, "The Great Transformation of Tibet? Rapid Labor Transitions in Times of Rapid Growth in the Tibet Autonomous Region," Himalaya, vol. 30, issue 1-2 (2010), pp. 63-79.

62"Dilemma of Development: Tibet's Development Project and Reductionist Reading,"tibetpolicy.net , (accessed June 29, 2017), http://tibetpolicy.net/comments-briefs/dilemma-of-development-tibets-development-project-and-reductionist-reading/

63 China's official nomination to UNESCO, p 137 of hard copy document seen by Gabriel Lafitte, and cited in his blog posted on October 18, 2016, http://rukor.org/in-the-no-mans-land-of-tibet

64 Nomads in 'no man's land': China's nomination for UNESCO World heritage risks imperilling Tibetans and wildlife, International Campaign for Tibet, June 30,2017, https://www.savetibet.org/nomads-in-no-mans-land-chinas-nomination-for-unesco-world-heritage-risks-imperilling-tibetans-and-wildlife-2/ (accessed June 30, 2017)

65 Blog by Gabriel Lafitte, http://rukor.org/in-the-no-mans-land-

of-tibet/, posted on October 18, 2016

66 The 'Ten-Year Master Plan' for the future of tourism in the Tibet Autonomous Region (2010-2020) defines the new 'zones', with Lhasa as the hub, as follows: "Tibet's tourism layout will include: the human culture tourism centre Lhasa and the ecotourism centre Nyingchi (Kongpo, Chinese: Linzhi, Tibet Autonomous Region); east-west tourism development axis and south-north tourism development axis that can connect Tibet with the outside; four boutique tourist routes in east, west, south, and north; seven scenic areas." The report also states that "tourist development axes will spread north, south, east and west from Lhasa" enabling fulfilment of the targets

Population Transfer and Western China 'Development' Program

1 *Mao: The Unknown Story.* p.552

2 as quoted in *Tibet Under Communist China: 50 Years.* p.45

3 *Tibet and the People's Republic: a report to the International Commission of Jurists.* p.289

4 *New Majority: Chinese Population Transfer Into Tibet.* p.38

5 for more see *Hungry Ghosts: China's Secret Famine*

6 as quoted in Peter Hessler's *Tibet Through Chinese Eyes* published in *The Atlantic Online.* February 1999. Available at: www.atlantic.com

7 *New Majority: Chinese Population Transfer into Tibet.* p.47

8 as quoted in *Tibet Under Communist China: 50 Years.* p.47

9 *Tibet Under Communist China: 50 Years.* p.47

10 ibid

11 as quoted in *Tibet Under Communist China: 50 Years.* p.47

12 *Beijing Review.* January 21-27 1991.

13 *Tibet Under Communist China: 50 Years.* p.48

14 as quoted in *Response to Beijing's Comments on De-militarization and 'Ethnic Cleansing'.* 5 September 2009. Available at: www.tibet.net

15 *Tibet Under Communist China: 50 Years.* p.47

16 as quoted in *New Majority: Chinese Population Transfer into Tibet.* p.54

17 for more see *Cutting Off Serpent's Head.* TIN/HRW. 1996; and *Tibet: Human Rights and Rule of Law.* ICJ. 1997.

18 for more see *Destruction by Design: Housing Rights Violations in Tibet*

by Scott Leckie

19 as quoted in *New Majority*. p.55

20 *Tracking the Steel Dragon*. p.9

21 ibid p.37

22 see 'The Second Invasion' in *Tracking the Steel Dragon*. pp.37-60

23 *The Poverty of Plenty*. p.vx

24 ibid xiii

25 *China's Great Leap Westward*. p.5

27 ibid p.6

27 ibid; also see *China Daily*. 18 September 2000

28 *Newsweek International*. 2 July 2000.

29 as quoted in *Height of Darkness: Chinese Colonialism on the World's Roof*. 10 December 2001.

30 see *Tibetan Bulletin*. July-August 2000.

31 *Written in Blood*. pp.105-108

32 for more see *New Majority*

33 see *An Investigative Report Into the Social and Economic Causes of the 3.14 Incident in Tibetan Areas. Gongmeng Law Research Center*.

34 *Tibet Daily*. 27 February 1991.

35 see *Destruction by Design: Housing Rights Violations in Tibet*. pp.85-113

36 *Tibet Through Chinese Eyes* (part 1, 2 & 3) by Peter Hessler. Available at: *The Atlantic Online* www.theatlantic.com

37 see *New Majority: Chinese Population Transfer into Tibet*. pp.101-145

38 Yeh Emily T. *Tamming Tibet*. Cornell University Press. Ithaca & London. 2013

39 http://www.chinafile.com/contributors/james-leibold

40 འབའ་པ་ཕུན་ཚོགས་དབང་རྒྱལ་གྱིས། རང་རྒྱལ་གྱི་མི་རིགས་གནད་དོན་དང་མི་རིགས་ལས་དོན་སྐོར་གྱི་ཕྱིར་རྟོག་ཁ་བ་དཀར་པོ་བོད་ཀྱི་རིག་གཞུང་ཞིབ་འཇུག་གིས་ཕྱི་ལོ་ ༢༠༡༢ བོར་པར་དུ་བསྐྲུན།

41 Bulag Uradyn E. *Municipalization and Ethnopolitics in Inner Mongolia. Mongols From Country to City*. in Ole Bruun and Li Narangoa (eds.) APD Singapore Pte Ltd. 2011

42 Circular of the State Council's General Office on the *Distribution of Suggestions on the Implementation of Policies and Measures Pertaining to the*

Development of the Western Region. Submitted by the Western Region Development Office of the State Council, September 29, 2001

43 http://www.straitstimes.com/asia/east-asia/beijing-finally-adopts-hukou-reforms

44 Nyima Tashi. *Development Discourses on the Tibetan Plateau: Urbanisation and Expropriation of Farmland in Dartsedo.* Himalaya. The Journal of the Association for Nepal and Himalayan Studies: Vol. 30: No. 1, Article 16

45 Jun Xu. *Challenges: Resettlement of Nomads in Qinghai Province.* Presented detailed paper at SLTP Conference, Leipzig, Dec. 2-3, 2009

46 https:// chinachange.org/2013/08/08/the-urban-grid-management-and-police-state-in-china-a-brief-overview/

47 https://www.hrw.org/news/2013/03/20/china-alarming-new-surveillance-security-tibet

48 The World Bank & Development Research Center of the State Council, the People's Republic of China. *Urban China toward Efficient, Inclusive, and Sustainable Urbanisation.* Washington DC, 2014

49 Zhao, B. 2005. *How to address the problem of land-lost farmers?* Renminwang, December, 9, 2005 <http://theory.people.com.cn/ GB/40553/3929253.html

50 http://news.xinhuanet.com/english/2015-08/26/c_134557687.htm

51 *Tibet Under Communist China: 50 Years.* p.i

52 *Mining in Tibet – mineral exploitation in Tibetan areas of the PRC.* p.84

53 Lhasang Tsering in *Sun Behind the Cloud,* a documentary on Tibetan struggle for freedom by Tenzing Sonam and Ritu Sarin

BIBLIOGRAPHY

An Investigative report into the social and economic causes of the 3.14 incident in Tibetan area. Research: Li Kun, Huang Li. Li Xiang, Wang Hong-zhe. Gongmeng Law Firm. 2008

Barnett, Robert. *The Chinese Frontiersman and the Winter Works - Chen Kuiyuan in the TAR, 1992-2000.* Paper presented at the History of Tibet Seminar, St Andrew's University, Scotland, August 2001

Barnnett, Robert and Akiner, Shirin. *Resistance and Reform in Tibet.* Motilal Banarsidass Publishers, New Delhi. 1996.

Bass, Catriona. *Education in Tibet: policy and practice since 1950.* Tibet Information Network and Zed books. London and New York. 1998

Becker, Jasper. *Hungry Ghosts: China's Secret Famine.* John Murray Publisher. London. 1997

Brox, Trine. *Tibetan Cultural as Battlefield: how the term 'Tibetan Culture' is utilized as political strategy.* Universitat Kopenhagen

Chang, Jung and Halliday, Jon. *Mao: the Unknown Story.* Vintage Books. London. 2006

China Perspectives No. 79 2009/3. *Special Feature, The Deadlock in Tibet.* Quarterly journal (sister publication of Perspective chinoises) published by CEFC

China's Tibet, a bimonthly of Tibetan News & Views. 2009.3 Vol. 20. Beijing, China

Choedon, Dhondup. *Life in the Red Flag People's Commune.* Translated and published by The Information Office of HH the Dalai Lama. Dharamsala. India. 1978

Coleman, Graham. *Handbook of Tibetan Culture: A Guide to Tibetan Centres and Resources Throughout World.* Published Rider. 1993

Crossette, Barbara. *So Close to Heaven: The Vanishing Buddhist Kingdoms of the Himalayas.* Alfred A. Knopf. 1995

Department of Information and International Relations. *The Mongols and Tibet: A Historical Assessment of Relations Between the Mongol Empire and Tibet.* DIIR. Dharamsala.

Department of Information and International Relations. *Tibet Under Communist China: 50 Years.* Dharamsala. 2001.

136

Drungtso, Tsering Thackchoe. *Tibetan Medicine: the healing science of Tibet.* Drungtso Publications. Dharamsala. 2006

Dunham, Mikel. *Buddha's Warriors, The Story of the CIA-backed Tibetan Freedom Fighters, the Chinese Invasion, and the Ultimate Fall of Tibet.* Jeremy P. Tarcher/Penguin. New York. 2004

Fan, Maureen. *For China's Nomads, Relocation Proves a Mixed Blessing More Opportunities, But Loss of Control.* Washington Post Foreign Service. 20 September, 2008

Fields, Rick. *How the Swans Came to the Lakes: a narrative history of Buddhism in America.* Shambhala Publications. 1992

Goldstein, Melvyn C., Dawai Sherap and Seibenschuh, Willaim R. *A Tibetan Revolutionary, the political life and times of Baba Phuntsok Wangye.* University of California Press. London. 2004

Gyatso, Palden with Shakya Tsering. *Fire Under Snow.*

Hessler, Peter. *Tibet Through Chinese Eyes.* Published in The Atlantic Online. February 1999. Available at http://www.theatlantic.com/past/issues/99feb/tibet.htm

Human Right Watch. *No One Has the Liberty to Refuse: Tibetan Herders Forcibly Relocated in Gansu, Qinghai, Sichuan, and Tibetan Autonomous Region.* Volume 19, No. 8 (c). June 2007

International Campaign for Tibet. *A Raging Storm: The Crackdown on Tibetan Writers and Artists after Tibet's Spring 2008 Protests.* Washington, DC. 2010

International Campaign for Tibet. *The Communist Party as Living Buddha, the crisis facing Tibetan religion under Chinese control.* Washington, DC. 2007

International Campaign for Tibet. *Crossing The Line: China's railway to Lhasa, Tibet.* Washington, DC.

International Campaign for Tibet. *Forbidden Freedoms: Beijing's Control of Religion in Tibet.* Washington, DC. 1990

International Campaign for Tibet. *Like Gold That Fears No Fire: new writing from Tibet.* Washington, DC. 2009

International Campaign for Tibet. *Tibet at a Turning Point: the spring uprising and China's new crackdown.* Washington, DC. 2008

International Campaign for Tibet. *Tracking the Steel Dragon: how China's economic policies and the railway are transforming Tibet.* Washington,

DC.

International Commission of Jurists. *The Question of Tibet and Rule of Law.* 1959

International Commission of Jurists. *Tibet and the People's Republic of China: a report to the international commission of jurists by its Legal Inquiry Committee on Tibet.* 1960.

International Commission of Jurists. *Tibet: Human Rights and the Rule of Law.* 1997

Jian, Ma. *Stick Out Your Tongue.* Translated from the Chinese by Flora Drew. Published by Chatto & Windus. London. 2006

Jigme, Gartse. *Tsenpoi Nyingtop (The Fierce Courage) Book-1.* Published by the International Campaign for Tibet. 2007.

Jintao, Hu. Speech at the Rally in Celebration of the 50th Anniversary of the Peaceful Liberation of Tibet. 19 July, 2001

Jinxiang, Zhou. Jun, Yang. Gong Peng. *Constructing a green railway on the Tibet Plateau: Evaluating the effectiveness of mitigation measures.* Transportation Research Part D. Available at www.elsevier.com/locate/trd

Laffitt, Gabriel. *China's Rise and the Rising Tibetan Nationalism* (texts of discussions held in DIIR's Lhakpa Tsering Memorial Hall in Dharamsala from 17-20 November 2009)

Lama, Dalai. *My Land My People.* Potala Publications. New York.

Limkin, Raphael. *Axis Rule in Occupied Europe: Occupation, Analysis of Governments, Proposal for Redress.* Carnegie Endowments for International Peace. Washington, DC. 1944

Lixiong,Wang and Shakya, Tsering. *The Struggle for Tibet.* Verso Books. New York. 2009

Lockie, Scott. *Destruction by Design: Housing Rights Violations in Tibet.* Centre on Housing Rights and Evictions (COHRE), The Netherlands. 1994.

Mirsky, Jonathan. *China's Gaping Wound.* The New Statemen. 4 June, 2007

Morton, Katherine. *Climate Change on the Tibetan Plateau: A New Security Challenge.* Woodrow Wilson Center, Washington DC. 12 February, 2009. Available at http://www.wilsoncenter.org/ondemand/index.cfm?fuseaction=Media.play&mediaid=A98B9EA0-B257-1FBB-7079F3FB8A24667F

Norbu, Jamyang. *High Sanctuary, wildlife and nature conservatory in Old Tibet.* 6 December, 2009. Available at www.shadowtibet.com

Norbu, Jamyang. *Shadow Tibet, Selected Writings 1989 to 2004.* Bluejay Books. New Delhi. 2004

Norbu, Namkhai. *Drung, Deu and Bon: Narrations, Symbolic Languages and the Bon Tradition in Ancient Tibet.* Library of Tibetan Works and Archives. Dharamsala.

Norbu, Namkhai. *Necklace of Dzi: A Cultural History of Tibet.* Library of Tibetan Works and Archives.

Nueden, Lodoe. *Nagtsang Shilui Kyiduk (Sufferings of the Nagtsang Boy).* Edited and Published by Khawa Karpo Tibetan Cultural Centre. Dharamsala. 2008

Order No. Five. State Religious Affairs Bureau Order. Issued by the People's Republic of China on 1 September 2007.

Rinpoche, Arjia. *Surviging the Dragon: a Tibetan lama's account of 40 years under Chinese rule.* Rodale Books. New York. 2010

Rinpoche, Sogyal. *The Tibetan Book of Living and Dying.* Revised and updated edition published by HarperSanFrancisco. 2002

Samten, Muge. (translated by Sangay Tandar Naga). *A History of Traditional Fields of Learning: a concise history of dissemination of traditional fields of leaning in Tibet.* Library of Tibetan Works & Archives. Dharamsala. 2005

Sen, Amartya. *The Argumentative Indian: Writing on Indian Culture, History and Identity.* Penguin Books. London. 2005

Shakabpa, Tsepon W.D. *Tibet: Political History.* Potala Publications. New York.

Shakya, Tsering. *Dragon in the Land of Snow, a history of modern Tibet since 1947.* Columbia University Press. New York. 1999

Shogdung or Tagyal. *Namsa Gojey - sa ji zhi bai sarjey la dris (The Line Between Sky and Earth - written for 2008 peaceful revolution).* Published by Doemey Tsengol Dengyab Nadrel and Domey Regional Standing Committee. 2010

Smith, Warren J. *China's Tibet? Autonomy or Assimilation.* Rowman & Littlefield Publishers. Maryland. 2008

Snellgrove, David and Richardson, Hugh. *A Cultural History of Tibet.* George Weidenfeld & Nicholson Ltd. London. 1968

Sonam, Tenzing and Sarin, Ritu. *The Sun Behind the Clouds: Tibet's Struggle for Freedom.* An award-winning documentary film by White Crane Films. 2009

Stein, R.A. Translated by J. E. Stapleton Driver. *Tibetan Civilization.* Faber and Faber Ltd. 1972

The Law Association for Asia & the Pacific Human Rights Standing Committee, and Tibet Information Network. *Defying the Dragon - China and Human Rights in Tibet.* London. March 1991

Theurang or Tashi Rabten. *Trag Yig (Written in Blood).* Published by Kirti Monastery. Dharamsala. 2009

Tibet Autonomous' Policy Research Office. (internal document) *cik dgu gya bzhi lor krung dbyang hru'u ci khru'u nas skong tshogs gnang ba'i bod kyi las don skor gyi bzhugs mol tshogs 'du'i dgongs don lag bstar byed pa'i rang skyong ljongs kyi yig cha 'dems sgarig. stod cha. (A collection of documents regarding carrying out of the ideals of Tibet Work Forum in presided over by the Party Secretary of the Central Government in 1984 - first part)* October 1984

Tibet Autonomous Regions' People's Press. *dus rabs gsar par skyod p'i gser zam - bod kyi las don skor gyi bzugs mol tshogs 'du thengs gsum pa'i dgongs don sgrog shyang 'grel bshad kyi dpyad gzhi (A Golden Bridge Leading to New Era — a reference book explaining the ideals of the Third Work Forum on Tibet)* Compiled by the TAR Communist Party's Propaganda Office. September 1994

Tibet Information Network. *A Poisoned Arrow: The Secret Report of the 10th Panchen Lama.* London. 1997

Tibet Information Network. *Mining Tibet: mineral exploitation in Tibetan areas of the PRC.* London. 2002

Tibet Information Network. *Sea of Bitterness: patriotic education in Qinghai Monasteries.* London. 1999.

Tibet Information Network. *Unity and Discord: music and politics in contemporary Tibet.* London. 1994

Tibet's Situation and Education in Primary Duties. A confidential report published by TAR People's Liberation Army's Political Bureau. 1 October 1960.

Tibet Support Group, UK. *New Majority: Chinese population transfer into Tibet.* Published by Tibet Support Group, UK. London. July 1995

Tibetan Centre for Human Rights and Democracy. *"Strike Hard Campaign" China's crackdown on political dissidence.* TCHRD. Dharamsala. December 2004

Tibetan Centre for Human Rights and Democracy. *Human Rights Situation in Tibet: Annual Report 2008.* Dharamsala. January 2009

Tibetan Centre for Human Rights and Democracy. *Human Rights Situation in Tibet: Annual Report 2009. TCHRD.* Dharamsala. January 2010-04-30

Tibetan Centre for Human Rights and Democracy. *State of Education in Tibet: a human rights perspective.* TCHRD. Dharamsala

Tibetan Information Network & Human Rights Watch/Asia. *Cutting Off Serpent's Head: tightening control in Tibet, 1994-1995.* London. March 1996

Tucci, Giuseppe. translated by J. E. Stapleton Driver. *Tibet: The Land of Snow.* Oxford & IBH Publishing Co. New Delhi. 1993

Tulku, Keutsang. *Memoirs of Keutsang Lama.* Paljor Publications. New Delhi. 2002

United States Commission on International Religious Freedom. *Annual Report 2009.* US Commission on International Religious Freedom. Washington, DC. May 2009

Wangyal, Dr Lobsang. *My Land My Culture.* Ridak Publications. Dharamsala. 2007

Watts, Jonathan. *Fungus gold rush in Tibetan plateau rebuilding lives after earthquake.* 17 June 2010. *The Guardian.*

Watts, Jonathan. *When a Billion Chinese Jump – How China will Save Mankind – or Destroy It.* Faber and Faber. 2010

Woeser. *GSAR RJE: bkag sdom byas pa'i bod kyi rig gnas gsar brje'i dran tho* (REVOLUTION: Banned memories of the Cultural Revolution in Tibet). Photographs by Tsering Dorjee. Translated by Dolkar. Published by the Norwegian Committee on Tibet. December 2009.

Woeser. *Tibet's True Heart: Selected Poems* translated by A. E. Clark. Ragged Banner Press. 2008

UN Declaration on the Rights of Indigenous Peoples. Adopted by General Assembly Resolution 13/295 on 13 September 2007